# THE ASSESSMENT OF MORALITY

-5.

# THE ASSESSMENT OF MORALITY

JOHN WILSON

Department of Educational Studies,
Oxford University

NFER Publishing Company Ltd.

Published by the NFER Publishing Company Ltd.
Book Division: 2 Jennings Buildings, Thames Avenue,
Windsor, Berks, SL4 1QS

Registered Office: The Mere, Upton Park, Slough, Bucks, SL1 2DQ

First Published 1973
© John Wilson, 1973

✓ SBN 85633  012  4

C:O7867

Printed in Great Britain by
Staples Printers Limited, at the Stanhope Press, Rochester, Kent

# Contents

# Preface

This book is intended primarily for research workers in psychology and the social sciences, although I do not intend by any means to exclude teachers, administrators, politicians and others who are concerned in a practical way with morality and moral education. Even if one is not engaged in research oneself, it is important to know something about this area, for it is obvious that we shall make no serious progress, either with the research or the practice of moral education, unless we first establish adequate methods of assessment.

It should also be obvious (but is not to all) that the difficulties of assessment are, and will continue for some time to be, as much conceptual as empirical. In the last few decades there has been enough philosophical literature, both of high quality and directly related to empirical research, to make it surprising that empirical researchers pay so little attention to philosophers. It is also true, however, that too much philosophical criticism has been purely destructive. I have tried to do something towards setting right both these mistakes in my *Philosophy and Educational Research* (1972), which deals with the application of conceptual questions to areas of psychological research. The present book may be seen as an off-shoot of this work inasmuch as it deals specifically and more fully with one particular area: the area of morality and moral education.

In an important sense, the book is a product of the first seven years of research, when I and my colleagues in psychology and the social sciences were collectively compelled to take the first steps in this field. I had to learn some psychology, and they some philosophy, the hard way. Together, we had to decide on definitions and assessment-methods before engaging in experimentation and other forms of practical work. The intertwining of conceptual and empirical considerations was particularly evident in the early stages, during which we had to familiarize ourselves with the literature and try to grasp the relevance of past research. Occasionally (as it seemed to us) our grasp picked up bits of solid gold; sometimes what we grasped turned out to be empty air; more often than either, we came up with a confused lump of something which might or might not have contained the precious metal. In general, there was so much confusion (together with so much promise) in this area that we thought it worthwhile to put this book together. Since most of the confusion is conceptual, I had the job of writing it: but it could not have been written without this corporate effort.

The book is intended as a basis for any empirical researcher in the area of morality and moral education, from the point of view of assessment. The difficulty with such a book lies in determining how far to go in the process of sketching out, or commenting upon, actual research projects, in particular the development of tests and assessment methods with which we shall be concerned in Part II. It would be ridiculous of me to propose detailed practical projects which would certainly fail for empirical reasons, reasons perhaps obvious to skilled psychologists but overlooked by me. On the other hand, if I am to avoid sins of omission and to say something constructive, I am bound to go into some detail, to say at least: 'This is the *sort* of thing that ought to be done'. So I shall try to resist the temptation of 'pure' philosophy, and put at least one foot into the empirical camp. This may well cause dissatisfaction, both among the 'pure' philosophers and among the psychologists. But one can't make an omelette without breaking egg-heads; and if somebody can do this particular (very important) job better, I shall be the first to applaud.

I have many critics to thank, too numerous to mention individually; but I have a particular debt of gratitude to those responsible for setting up the Research Unit, and to my colleagues in it for many fruitful conversations.

Finally, readers may like to know that we shall be continuing this research under the sponsorship of the Warborough Trust, in conjunction with the Oxford University Department of Educational Studies.

J. B. W.

Oxford 1972.

NOTE
I use the following abbreviations in footnotes:
*Introduction to Moral Education* (Wilson 1968))—IME
*Education in Religion and the Emotions* (Wilson (1971))—ERE
*Philosophy and Educational Research* (Wilson (1972))—PER
Full details of these and other works are given in the bibliography.

# Plan

The assessment of morality is a vast topic, and I must here say something about what sort of ground I intend to cover.

## Normative and non-normative research

Some types of research, among them research in an area for which 'moral education' may stand as a convenient general title, are intended not only to establish what *is* the case: they are also intended to assess what is the case in terms of what *ought* to be the case, and to discover methods of moving the former nearer to the latter. The researcher is concerned not only to determine what the morality of various people or 'subjects' (Ses[1]) actually is: but also to determine how far it falls short of what it ought to be. Research of this kind needs to be clearly demarcated, because its interests require a significantly different methodology I shall give it a grand name and call it 'normative'.

That research in moral education[2] is normative, in the sense described, is a matter of simple logic. The morally educated S must be an *improvement* on the morally uneducated S: this is part of the meaning of 'morally educated'. The researcher must therefore begin by establishing the norms of his (normative) research: that is, what it *means* to be 'morally educated', or educated in the area of morality. I have tried to do this at length elsewhere,[3] and shall not repeat it here. Then he must turn his attention to methods of assessment, which is what I shall be doing in this book: and only then, having established proper methods of assessment and experimented sufficiently with their help, can he pronounce on what moves ought to be made in educational practice.

1. I shall use this abbreviation throughout.
2. Indeed all genuine research in education, if by 'education' we understand anything like the concept outlined by Peters (1966), or think that people who are educated must (logically) have been *improved* in some way. See PER, p. 2 ff.
3. IME, Chs. 1–4: ERE, Ch. 6. The reader who has basic philosophical doubts should consult these works: but knowledge of them is not essential to this book.

Serious normative research in morality, however, is a comparative newcomer; and it should in principle connect with a fairly long tradition of non-normative research which goes back to Piaget and beyond. The non-normative researcher, of course, is not necessarily concerned with moral *education* at all. Typically his work has been carried on under such (mystifying) titles as 'moral development', 'socialization', 'the growth of moral concepts', 'character studies', and so on. These titles represent attempts to determine what the morality of various Ses is, and why it is; and plainly this ought to be of great importance to the researcher in moral education.

In practice, however, this is not the case (although many think it is). There are a number of basic methodological difficulties, or philosophical difficulties, about nearly all non-normative research in this area, and these make it very unclear, to me at least, just *what* has been established. There are problems about what phenomena we are to include under 'morality': about how to delimit the area of morality. Most empirical workers have not faced these at all. Then there are difficulties about the 'cognitive' aspects of morality, about the notions of 'moral development' and 'stages of development' (titles under which the main stream of work, at least in the post-Piagetian tradition, has been done). These lead us at once to more basic difficulties about the nature of the 'ground level' data on which researchers have worked. Similar difficulties crop up with the 'affective' or 'motivational' aspects.

I shall begin by dealing with the above, both in general and by looking at one or two actual pieces of work. I cannot do this as fully as might for other purposes be desirable, and I certainly cannot attempt a general survey of work in this area, but I hope to achieve my main purpose, which is to make clear where the main methodological difficulties lie, and why it is that we know so little. This leads, at the end of Part I, to a more general and constructive consideration of the assessment of morality, and to the necessity for a more sophisticated set of concepts or 'moral components' with which to work. In Part II we shall be concerned specifically with normative research ('moral education'): we shall examine the components in some detail, and go on to consider methods and forms of assessment in a fairly practical way. I stop at the point where I think that the competent and philosophically-informed empirical researcher can take over.

# Part I
## Definitions and Problems
## 1. Defining the moral area

### A.  The importance of definition

A great many books and articles have appeared (many of them recently) by psychologists and other empirical workers which include 'moral' or 'morality' in their titles. These words, like other research-titles ('intelligence', 'prejudice', 'altruism', etc.), represent concepts which in turn group together phenomena in the 'real world'—I mean, the world outside the researcher's study or laboratory—in which we have some practical or theoretical interest. We are practically interested, perhaps, in advancing the cause of 'moral education'; or, more theoretically, in 'the morality' of adolescents in Birmingham or Bangkok. It is therefore of some importance to know what we mean by such terms, and what the researchers mean by them.

Actually, very few researchers deal overtly with this problem at all. We are left to recreate their unconscious concept of morality from their empirical work. Sometimes psychological writers talk overtly about 'the definition' or 'the concept' of so-and-so. On first looking at this brand of psychological literature, one may optimistically suppose that the authors are really concerned with the *meaning* of the terms which appear in their research-titles, but one will usually be disappointed.

What usually goes wrong[1] is the failure to distinguish between questions of the form 'What is the meaning of "X"?', where we put X inside inverted commas in order to keep ourselves firmly in the realm of meaning and definitions, and questions of the form 'What is the nature of X?', where we are asking about the *thing* X and not the *word* 'X'. Both types of questions can take the form of 'What is X?', this being *either* a demand for information about what the word 'X' means, *or* a demand for information about the nature of the thing X itself. Usually, psychologists are interested in the second, not the first. They want to know what the 'things'

1. See PER, Section 3.

(intelligence, attitudes, etc.) *are*: how they work, the details of their mechanisms, their functions and 'development', the phenomena they generate, and so on. This is a perfectly legitimate interest, but it should not masquerade as an interest in meaning, definitions or concepts.

Some psychologists might say something like, 'It is not our interest or our job to investigate the meanings of terms: we leave that to the philosophers. When we talk of "intelligence", "attitudes", etc. we are not concerned with meanings at all, only with the phenomena: we may occasionally produce a "stipulative" or "operational" definition, but our only interest is to establish facts: empirical co-variances between certain behavioural performances and certain other performances (say, performance on an IQ test and performance in school examinations)'. Is there anything wrong with this? We might, I think, begin by being somewhat surprised that they eschewed *all* interest in normal meanings, for presumably it is *some* concept of intelligence, *some* meaning of 'intelligent', that leads them to make certain investigations and not other investigations, to construct tests of one kind rather than another, and so on. Of course, it is possible to say 'Intelligence tests, and work in the area we call "intelligence", do not necessarily have *anything* to do with the normal meaning of "intelligent": work in the area we call "prejudice" and tests of "racial prejudice" have *nothing* necessarily to do with the word "prejudice" as normally used', and so on, but it sounds rather extreme.

I do not know just how many psychologists would be prepared to take this extreme view: usually they dither.[1] But in any case, there is a price to be paid: the price of leaving a horrifying gap between these 'empirical co-variances' and the normal meaning of terms in everyday usage. The question arises, 'How far is what psychologists mean, or appear to mean, by "intelligence", "emotion", "morality", "altruism", etc. coextensive with what these terms usually mean?' Now they may, sometimes, be fairly coextensive; the gap may sometimes not be large. But the gap is horrifying because it *may* be large and—more important—*because we cannot tell how large it is without looking: and this sort of 'looking' is a conceptual or philosophical business.*

---

1. Cruel but true. Many start by claiming that they are dealing with (say) 'emotion' in its normal sense. Under pressure (e.g. have they done justice to *beliefs*, which are an integral part of emotions?) they retreat and say that their work is 'purely empirical', 'scientific', 'concerned with co-variances', etc. Then they may backslide and claim that their work is about what 'emotion' normally means after all, or that 'emotion' *ought* to mean what they say, or almost anything.

*Prima facie* we are interested in intelligence, morality, etc. in the normal meaning of those terms. We may not be clear—and here we need conceptual or philosophical ability—just what we *do* mean by them: but we are sure, and rightly, that it is *this* meaning that concerns us, and not just any meaning that may be attached to them by psychologists or anyone else. This is not just a matter of linguistic fussiness. When we want our children to be 'educated', 'altruistic', 'intelligent', etc. we refer (albeit vaguely) to a world of human interests which are reflected by ordinary human usage: this is why ordinary usage is important, at least as a starting-off point; not because philosophers like to play with words.

Unfortunately, there is no short cut to the kind of clarity we need here. It is no good producing 'operational definitions' or 'working definitions': the gap between these and the proper or correct definitions—that is, the proper description of our interests in verbal form—still has to be inspected. Equally it is no good conducting a sort of poll which will tell us what various people or classes of people say that they mean by various words—for they may *think they know, but be wrong.* This is the first lesson in philosophy, taught by Socrates and his successors: indeed philosophy could not exist, were it not that we can use a word correctly in everyday speech, yet not be clear about the rules for its use. So researchers cannot avoid the initial conceptual task.

Of course, this does not commit us to saying that researchers should not use technical terms, or that they should not sometimes withdraw from the 'normal-language' world of human interests into a world of 'constructs'. As in the case of the physical sciences, this may ultimately be very useful: empirical co-variances which need not be described or even describable in ordinary English—for instance, those in sub-atomic physics—may turn out to be of immense practical importance. But *at some point* they will have to be married up to our interests. If physics did not bear on descriptions like 'a destructive explosion', 'providing power for a million homes', or 'reaching the moon', it would be a mere game. It is the area in which the marriage takes place that requires attention.

## B. The area of 'morality'

It does not need great philosophical expertise to appreciate that 'morality' and 'moral' are likely to be even more liable to confusion than 'intelligence' and 'intelligent'. To repeat: the initial question for all researchers in this field is not 'What is morality?' in the sense of 'What does morality consist of (what is its essence, how does it function)?', but rather 'What are we going to *count as* "moral" or "morality"—what are we going to *mean by* these terms?'

Of course there are not necessarily 'right answers' to such questions, and, anyway, it is always open to people to use terms as they like. A researcher could say, for instance, 'By "morality" I mean "the principles of the Ten Commandments": by "moral" I mean "Whatever (judgements and behaviour) is in accordance with the Ten Commandments".' Then so long as this researcher is consistent in this use, and so long as these phrases are themselves clear—so long as we always know what to count as 'the Ten Commandments' and 'in accordance with the Ten Commandments' —at least we know where we are: we know what his research is supposed to be *about*. We may still object that this is not what 'moral' and 'morality' normally mean, but this is a lesser disadvantage and not so disastrous as lack of clarity.

It is of course *a* disadvantage, and likely to mislead the researcher as well as his audience. But terms like 'moral' may be ambiguous, or vague, or be used differently by different English-speaking groups, so that it would be rash to talk of *the* 'normal meaning'.[1] Moreover, at some stage the problem will arise of how to translate our research-titles satisfactorily into other languages. What we require is not so much the (sometimes over-fussy) 'linguistic analysis' of the *words* as to establish a clear *concept* which can fairly be represented by 'moral' and 'morality', and by similar words in other languages. The only point of looking at the words is to establish the concept. Once we have an unambiguous concept— once we know, with complete clarity, what the rules and boundaries of the concept are, what we are going to count as cases of it and what we are going to exclude—then we can make this clear in any language and to any person.

Unfortunately, this is not so easy as it may sound. A reaction like 'Oh, well, if all you mean is that you have to define your terms clearly . . .' misses the point. For although we *can* count anything we like as 'morality' (though perhaps in rash defiance of normal usage) we are not clear about what we *want* to count. Thus one psychologist, in conversation, said that part of what he *meant by* 'moral' or 'mentally healthy' was 'well adjusted to one's job', 'finding satisfaction in one's work' and 'fitting into one's society'. 'But the Nazi who diligently drove Jews into gas chambers, and enjoyed it, fits these descriptions: do you want to call him "moral"?'

1. ERE ,Appendix VII: PER, Part I.

'Well, no, he's an exception'. 'Then you haven't got a consistent and clear concept of "moral"'. Note that this Socratic procedure does not bully the person into adopting the concept which 'philosophers' want him to have, nor is it just fussy 'linguistic analysis'. The point is that the person simply *is not clear about what concept he wants.*

That is why most psychologists do not even make the attempt. The person quoted above could have said that most people whom we want to call 'moral' also *in fact* find satisfaction in their work, fit into society, etc., and this may be true (though we should have *first* to decide whom we wanted to call 'moral' and why, and what was to count as 'fitting into society', etc. and *then* to find out the empirical facts). Yet he appeared to be giving a definition, or outlining a concept; although, in fact, he was not concerned with this but, rather, with certain possible contingent or factual correlations between 'moral' people and 'adjusted' people. Most of what psychologists have seemed to say about the concept of morality has not really been concerned with the *concept* at all. Partly for this reason (and partly not to weary the reader), I shall not devote very much space to a critical analysis of their writings on this topic, although I shall mention them *en passant* while having a look at some of the pitfalls.

Elsewhere[1] I have set out a simplified account of possible uses of 'moral' as follows:

A. 'Moral' (as contrasted with 'immoral'), is often used as a term of approval.

B. 'Moral' is used as a descriptive term, to classify a particular kind of action or belief. Its opposite here is simply 'not moral' or 'non-moral' (as when we say, 'It's not a moral issue, it's simply a matter of taste').

But this descriptive or classificatory sense can be based on different criteria and hence mean different things:

(i) It can be used in a 'sociological' sense. Sociologists and historians commonly talk about 'the morality' of a particular society or social group, about what counted as 'moral' or 'immoral' behaviour in ancient Sparta or during the Victorian age in England. Here we refer to a particular code, or set of *mores*. When we use these words with reference to our own society we often bring in sense A above, with its overtones of praise or blame: we say, 'that's a most immoral thing to do', meaning that it is against the current

1. IME, pp. 44–5.

moral code, and probably also implying our condemnation of the action.

(ii) It can be used to mark out a particular kind of human thought and action, not on the basis of what the *mores* of a particular society are, but on some other basis. Thus when we say 'The ancient Hebrews thought that whether or not you ate certain kinds of food was a moral issue, but I don't think it is', or 'What sort of clothes you wear isn't really a moral issue, it's a matter of taste', we are obviously not thinking just of what the *mores* of a particular society are. We seem rather to be making some kind of logical or conceptual classification of the area of morality, quite apart from what anyone seems to *regard* (rightly or wrongly) as that area.

Consider now B(i). In this sense, different social groups have different moralities, although sometimes the content will overlap. There are two approaches the researcher can make here. First, he can do a kind of descriptive anthropology or sociology, comparing (for instance) the 'honour ethic' of Homer's heroes with the more utilitarian *mores* of British businessmen, the asceticism of the early Christian monks, the stark Communism of ancient Sparta, and so on. Important and interesting though this work is, it does not seem wholly appropriate for the educational psychologist. Secondly, the researcher can make some more or less overt claim about some particular set of *mores* which *he* is going to count as 'morality'; and this, in fact, is what most psychologists have done. This also has its difficulties, however, as we shall see.

The chief difficulty, which I shall want to stress throughout this section, is the assumption that 'morality' must have a particular *content*. Researchers have assigned (usually unconsciously) some such content to 'morality' and proceeded to conduct their empirical inquiries on this basis. Very often they have done this with extreme naivety, and tacitly defined 'morality' in terms of what is considered to be 'moral' in their own society. Thus Havighurst and Taba (1949) inquired into five 'moral traits'—honesty, responsibility, loyalty, moral courage and friendliness; not all the items on this list would commend themselves to, for instance, a Japanese samurai, Machiavelli, or members of a tough teenage gang. The point comes out more strongly in their assessment methods: the researchers derived *reputation ratings* from peers, day-school teachers, Sunday-school teachers, youth leaders and employers—in other words, 'moral' is to mean 'what is thought to be good by the society (or the official "establishment" of the society)'. The same point applies to other studies, such as Hartshorne and May (1930), Peck and Havighurst (1960) and others too numerous to mention— indeed, to almost all work in this field.

Somewhat more sophisticated, but suffering from the same defect of allocating a particular content to 'morality', are studies like those of Piaget, Kohlberg, and other more recent writers. One of the more lucid accounts of this approach written by a psychologist is found in Derek Wright's *The Psychology of Moral Behaviour* (1971), an excellent work which nevertheless illustrates the defect very clearly. 'Moral behaviour', says Wright, 'consists of all the various things people do in connection with moral rules'.[1] It is very much to Wright's credit that he appreciates the importance of rules and reasons in morality, but, turning to his discussion of moral rules, we read: '. . . we can all recognize the difference between at one extreme the conventional rules of dress or eating and at the other those concerned with keeping promises, honesty, respect for the rights of the individual, and sympathy for those in need. Whether or not the former ever deserve to be called moral, the latter always do. . . . Moral rules are foundational in the sense that they are concerned with the maintenance of, for instance, trust, mutual help and justice in human relationships. Unless these exist in some measure it becomes virtually impossible to continue any social activity. It is therefore not surprising that, though conventions and customs vary widely from one society to another, basic moral principles apparently do not.'[2]

It is not absolutely clear whether the content given to 'morality' here is sociological (as in B(i) above) or logical (B(ii)). If we ask which rules are 'important' in the sense of 'taken very seriously by the social group', then we get different answers for different groups. The difference which Wright says 'we can all recognize', between 'conventional rules of dress or eating' and rules concerned with 'respect for the rights of the individual and sympathy for those in need' (are there *rules* about sympathy?), is that most people in our society regard the former as trivial and the latter as serious. But this is not true of societies which have important dress- or food-taboos, and which may not have anything like the same regard for human rights or sympathy as we have. This sort of difference— this sense of 'important'—is relative or culture-bound. On the other hand, if 'important' is taken (as I think the author wants to take it for most of the time) to mean 'necessary if there is to be any

1. Wright (1971), p. 15.
2. ibid., p. 13.

form of society at all', then the criterion may be a logical one. On this criterion it is not only 'not surprising' that moral principles 'apparently' do not vary widely: they (logically) could not, because there could not be any society without the principles.

This logical criterion (B(ii)) for morality is certainly a step further forward than any conventional or sociological one. Unfortunately, it is very unclear as to how it could be applied. We should first have to determine just what rules or principles were logically or empirically required by any society. Some philosophers[1] have claimed to show certain principles (notoriously, truth-telling[2]) to be logically required norms for any society—and one might add others, such as some elementary form of justice or contract-keeping, some kind of property-rules, and so on. But we are not clear about just what rules these are, or how many of them there are, and any attempt to determine what rules are *empirically* (rather than logically) necessary seems even more difficult. I do not say that we ought not to investigate the area further, but this does not commend itself as a workable criterion. Moreover, we should have to exclude from our researches any thought and action (very commonly called 'moral') which might be shown *not* logically or empirically necessary: for instance, research into morality supposedly derived from religion, various branches of sexual morality, and other moral ideals of a kind which might have little to do with the maintenance of society.

A much more determined, though also more confused, attempt to use a logical or formal criterion is apparent in Kohlberg's work. '. . . like most (?) moral philosophers from Kant to Hare, Baier, Aiken, etc., we define morality in terms of the formal character of a moral judgment or a moral point of view, rather than in terms of its content. Impersonality, ideality, universalizability, and pre-emptiveness are among the formal characteristics of a moral judgment'.[3] 'Unlike judgments of prudence or aesthetics, moral judgments tend to be (?) universal, inclusive, consistent, and grounded on objective, impersonal or ideal grounds.'[4] This enables us 'to define a moral judgment as "moral" without considering its content (the action judged) and without considering whether it agrees with our own judgments or standards'.[5]

1. See e.g., Winch (1959), also IME, p. 103 ff.
2. The argument is roughly: 'society' conceptually implies 'communication'; 'communication' conceptually implies a norm of truth-telling.
3. Kohlberg (1971), p. 55.
4. ibid., p. 56.
5. ibid., p. 57.

However, it is not really clear what this criterion is supposed to be. Our suspicions are aroused when Kohlberg outlaws statements like, 'It's not right to steal because you'll get put in jail': these are 'not moral judgments'.[1] The dismissal of 'judgments of prudence or aesthetics' suggests that Kohlberg is in fact using a criterion in terms of the *kind of reasons given:* the picture is of a class of 'moral' reasons (derived from or connected with justice, in Kohlberg's view)[2] alongside a class of 'prudential' or 'aesthetic' reasons. But it is, of course, perfectly possible to have 'prudential' or 'aesthetic' reasons which are impersonal, based on an ideal, and universalized (whatever the best interpretation of these terms may be). For instance, I may govern my behaviour and think that others should govern theirs by some kind of egoism, or by an 'honour ethic'. *Any* kind of reasons *can*, in point of strict logic, be used to back whatever behaviour I think it right for myself and others to engage in[3]—though it does not follow that all reasons are equally good.

We shall see later the effect that this confusion has on Kohlberg's assessment procedures. But we can already guess that his picture of morality (whether intentionally adopted or not) is, in fact, not content-free: it is a utilitarian picture based on justice—roughly, a basic 'social morality'. Hence, we are not surprised at such remarks as 'The most fundamental values of a society are termed moral, and the major moral values in our society are the values of justice',[4] 'A moral obligation is an obligation to respect the right or claim of another person',[5] 'A moral conflict is a conflict between competing claims of men',[5] and so forth. Despite his flirtation with a formal, content-free criterion, the content is plain enough.[7]

Kohlberg is only the most recent (and important) example of a fashionable tendency which needs to be clearly understood. Without lengthy quotation, it is fair to say that researchers have *not* been concerned with what children or adults think to be overridingly and prescriptively right or wrong in their lives generally (or with their general overriding behaviour), but rather with their thoughts, attitudes and behaviour in reference to highly specific situations— roughly, situations in which *public rules*, 'given', and usually backed

---

1. Kohlberg (1964), p. 405; cf. Kohlberg (1971), p. 56.
2. See Kohlberg (1970), *passim.*
3. I have spelled this out more fully in IME, p. 76 ff: ERE, Ch. 6.
4. Kohlberg (1970), p. 67.
5. ibid., p. 70.
6. Kohlberg (1971), p. 51.
7. Particularly in Kohlberg (1970).

up by the authority of parents or peers, are at stake. The importance
of this point merits expansion.

One author (who writes very lucidly about this area) says that
morality '. . . is learning to participate in a form of social life
regulated by a system of rules and expectations'.[1] Now if we have
this picture of morality as participation in existing rules, and/or
what the author describes as 'role-concepts' (father, doctor, shop-
keeper, motorist, etc.), then this will to a very great extent dictate
both the form and the findings of our research. It will now be
plausible to regard marble-playing as sufficiently analagous to
morality to justify inductions from the one to the other, and it will
be sensible to restrict our stories, interviews and so on to situations
in which public, authority-backed rules are at stake. We shall not,
however, be sure of discovering the overriding principles or behaviour of children in general: for what we have done is to put
children in a specific context where only certain kinds of reasons
and certain kinds of learning or 'development' will count. It is as if
we were trying to discover children's thinking and behaviour only
within a predetermined game or rule-structure (for instance, in
mathematics, or Sunday etiquette, or on the football field).

Much of the confusion here has arisen from the (again, often
tacit) belief that parental and social rules—i.e. externally-imposed
or 'given' rules—are the only rules which young children can
seriously be said to follow. I quote from a recent researcher[2]:
'Any morality is made up of a body of laws which become rules or
principles of conduct. The Greek term *nomos*, meaning "law",
therefore serves admirably as the basis of our terminology. We can
use it to define the four stages through which the child passes in
his moral development. He begins in a state of anomy—that is,
lawlessness—in the true sense of the word. Being without rules
governing behaviour, he is at the mercy of instinct and impulse.
Hence, secondly, the need of heteronomy, that is, rules imposed by
others. . . . The rules are external to him. . . . Without such heteronomy the child could not develop an inner morality of his own. . . .'

What seems odd here is that the notion of a rule is restricted to an
externally-imposed rule. I do not know if there is a particular
sense[3] of 'rule' of which this is true; but, if so, it is certainly not the
only sense. As soon as a child has the use of language, he also has
the power of forming intentions, adopting means to ends, and

---

1. Dearden (1968), pp. 168–9.
2. Bull (1969), p. 26.
3. *Sense*, not *type*. Of course there are *types* of rules of which it is true.

'following rules' in senses sufficiently clear described by many philosophers.[1] It is plainly ridiculous to imagine that, once armed with language, the child does not have wants of his own, and does not try to get what he wants by following rules and principles. Only by concentrating exclusively on the pressure of other people on the child to obey *their* rules could we ever find ourselves saying this.

But there are many other incentives to rule-following. The child has various wants which he must satisfy, and various emotions connected with these wants. From a very early age (certainly before the supposed 'heteronomous' stage) he feels such things as guilt, fear, anger, self-interested desire, love, hate, and many others. All these will involve him in behaviour which will be to some extent governed by his conceptual and empirical understanding of the world, and therefore rule-governed. He will learn that his mother comes when he cries, that to get warm he must go near, but not too near, to the fire, that to reach the jampot he must use a chair to stand on, that playing successfully with the cat necessitates certain things which he must do and certain things which he must not. Indeed, all that (large) part of his life which is not dictated by adults' and peers' insistence on his following public rules will be devoted to following rules—overriding and important rules—which arise from the interaction between the child's wants, his understanding of the environment and the environment itself.

It is true that to follow rules the child must have language: language-using and rule-following are conceptually (not just empirically) connected. And language—a further conceptual point—is necessarily something public, something the child must learn, not something he can make up entirely by himself. In this sense, the child is dependent on existing rule-structures in the adult world, since all such structures are themselves dependent on language; and, of course, in order to learn many things the child is similarly dependent: much that he will want to learn (or be induced by adults and peers to learn) already exists in such rule-structures. The child's learning will consist, as we are constantly (and on the whole rightly) told by some philosophers,[2] in his being initiated into various 'forms of thought', or rule-governed 'worthwhile activities', that already exist and are already (so to speak) publicly manned and controlled.

All this is true, and one can understand the temptation to

1. For a useful summary, see Black (1967).
2. Peters (1966).

assimilate morality to this model. To make it fit, however, we have to distort, not merely much of what in normal English we should describe as 'moral' or 'morality'—this hardly matters—but much of what, as empirical researchers, we need to look at in the child's thought and behaviour. For instance, learning to perform well in such areas as truth-telling, promise-keeping, and respecting property may fairly be described as 'learning to participate in a form of social life regulated by a system of rules and expectations'; but there are important moral virtues which simply do not fit this (courage, prudence, temperance), and many general rules and concepts which require general conceptual and empirical understanding to grasp, rather than participation 'in a form of social life'. Thus, the concept of others' interests, widely agreed by philosophers to be of importance to moral education, may be (as a matter of pedagogy) *approached via* specific forms of social participation, but does not logically rest upon them. This is to say nothing of the wider area of moral ideals and feelings which are in no sense 'social'. Only some extremist theory to the effect that individual decision is in very definite ways bounded by the language, concepts and social forms available (one version of which I have criticised elsewhere)[1] would make us hesitate to regard this account of morality as, at best, one-sided.

To summarize briefly: If we define (as most researchers have) the moral area in terms of a particular content or set of reasons, it will be difficult to do justice in our research to those whose over-riding principles and modes of thought do not fit the content or reasons. Suppose, for instance, that 'morality' for us is about justice, honesty, keeping contracts, helping our neighbours and so on—roughly, a utilitarian picture; and now suppose that we come up against a man whose overriding principles are those of a Japanese samurai, or of a tough teenage gang-member who is chiefly concerned with physical courage, not losing face, etc.—roughly, an 'honour ethic'. We shall be unlikely to grasp how he stands even in relation to our own narrow picture of 'morality', unless we grasp his overriding principles (which in many cases it would be absurd not to call 'moral').

1. ERE, Appendix VII: IME, pp. 117–8.

# 2. Problems of assessment: 'cognitive'

It is possible to see fairly clearly how this restricted picture of morality affects the assessment-methods commonly used by researchers. In this section we shall briefly consider the 'cognitive' assessments, or assessments of 'moral thinking' or 'moral judgement', as instantiated in the work of Kohlberg and others. I cannot, of course (and do not need to), go into great detail or do justice to the work of any single researcher: nevertheless the following points may shed some light on the difficulties.

1. First, the selection of assessment methods—Kohlberg's stories, for instance—will naturally be dictated by the (tacit) definition of morality in terms of a particular content. They will not necessarily tap the subject's (S's) overriding principles, which may fall outside that content. This obviously sets a limitation on the assessments: they cannot serve us if we are concerned to find out what are S's most important values, principles or behaviour-generating rules. (Already we feel tempted to say 'S's morality': a temptation to which, I shall argue later, we ought to yield.)

But this is more than a limitation. If we do not know what S's overriding principles are, how can we select the stories fairly? I mean this: It might be said, by Kohlberg and others, that all we want to know in this research is how S stands in relation to 'social morality' (justice and so forth). So we pick stories designed to elucidate this and see how S rates on these stories—what 'stage of development' he has reached. But how much *weight* S puts on this 'social morality' will depend on what the counter-attractions are, on the 'pulls' or distractions from other kinds of principles—principles of honour, or guilt, or self-advantage or whatever. Now unless we have a clear idea of what these other 'pulls' are, we cannot construct stories which incorporate them satisfactorily; and if we do not incorporate them, we cannot measure how S stands in relation to 'social morality'. We cannot tell what S really thinks he or another ought to do in a 'justice' situation, unless we build in possible conflicts produced by other 'pulls'—I would say, other kinds of morality.

It might be argued that the stories themselves (and, more plausibly, the lengthy interviews and other data that precede the story-construction) determine what the 'pulls' are. But this is not convincing. First, if we conceive of 'morality' as 'social morality', this will inevitably prejudice our collection of data, for we will perceive various 'pulls' only as connected with this social morality. Thus, the description of the supposed 'stages' is nearly always in terms of an S failing to get, or partly getting, or wholly getting the hang of social morality: e.g. S is concerned with 'performing good or right roles' (a case of partly getting the hang). The 'pulls' are not done justice to in their own right. Secondly, there will be 'pulls'—other overriding principles or types of morality—which may not conflict at all with social morality. 'Honour' may usually coincide with 'justice', or 'honour' may operate in areas where there is no possible conflict. The former case can be taken care of by a close inspection of the reasons for choice: does S think that the debt should be repaid because it is honourable, or because it is just? But the latter case is more difficult. Suppose S's morality—his overriding concerns—are with 'honour' or some other ego-ideal in an area which rarely or never conflicts with social morality: for instance, in the matter of religious observance, dress, various food taboos, etiquette, sex, and so forth? It might be hard here even to think of ways of measuring this concern against the concerns of social morality, particularly if S is a hermit, or a 'drop-out', or in some other way disconnected from society. We need, initially, a much more open and theory-free approach.

2. Secondly, if morality is construed and assessed on the model of a (serious) social 'game' which the growing child has to learn, then of course it is clear that (as with any game or rule-governed system) there will be 'stages' of learning. With the Piaget-Kohlberg conception, it could not (logically could not) be otherwise. Very roughly, the child moves from 'external, quasiphysical happenings' (Kohlberg's Level I), to 'performing good or right roles' and 'the conventional order' (Level II), to the notion of 'shared or shareable standards' or 'contractual orientation' (III).[1] But how could this be otherwise? What the child is doing here involves, and indeed partly consists in, an extension of conceptual sophistication: he moves from 'quasiphysical' *things*, to the more abstract world of 'roles', to the still more abstract world of people and principles.

1. Kohlberg (1970), pp. 71–2. Cf. Peters (1971).

There are (again briefly) logical or conceptual reasons for supposing that the general move from concrete to abstract, from the particular to the general, is inevitable: that is, it is not a matter for empirical discovery but a necessity of logic. Just as in chess one cannot—logically cannot—grasp the concept 'check-mate' before the concept 'check', or the concept 'check' before the concept 'king', so in 'social morality' it is hard to imagine a young child grasping abstract principles of universalized justice before grasping particular instances and roles. It is interesting and important to know at what ages various children make these moves; but the stages themselves are—if we interpret them in this light[1]— a matter of logic, not just empirical facts.

3. Thirdly, there are very serious problems about the language used in the assessments. I am not now referring to whether test-stories are constructed in the first or third person, or to the children's verbal ability, or to similar methodological (rather than conceptual) difficulties. I refer to the obvious fact that *we do not know what S means* when he uses words like 'right', 'ought', 'should', and so on, and that we cannot assign a 'stage' or type of reasoning to S unless and until we do know.

Thus, for one S, 'right' may actually *mean* 'approved by adults' or 'approved by peers'; for another, 'ought' may *mean* 'serving my

1. Peters (1971, p. 242) interprets Kohlberg as claiming that the order of stages 'could not be otherwise than it is because of the logical relationships between the concepts'. I do not myself think that Kohlberg is either clear or consistent about this and other claims: I do not know what he and other developmental theorists mean by 'stage'—what the stages are stages *of*—nor have I found clear and unambiguous criteria of allocation to different stages. But *if* we are talking about S's progressive *understanding* of certain types of rules and concepts (as in mathematics or chess), or *insofar* as we are talking about this (and not, e.g., about what rules and concepts S *prefers* to use), then obviously this understanding can be taught. Peters (p. 243 ff.) makes something like this point. But the discussion seems to me bedevilled by an uncritical approach to the whole notion of 'moral development': it is simply not clear what *type* of phenomena we are talking about. I hope to make this plainer below (see p. 16 ff., and Appendix III): but because of this confusion, time spent on a detailed analysis of particular 'theories of moral development' seems to me time ill-spent—for the purposes of the present book, anyway.

These and other points are not, of course, intended as an attack on Kohlberg (whose work is, in my view, the most extensive and interesting we have seen in the empirical area). One could not attack anyway, because it would not be clear what one was attacking. It will need many years' close co-operation and dialogue between philosophers and psychologists before such clarity can be achieved on both sides. The difficulties of such a dialogue are well illustrated in Beck (1972) and Mischel (1971). See also PER, Part I.

own advantage'; for another, 'good' may *mean* 'in accordance with the rules'. So if we ask these Ses what is right, or what they (or another) ought to do, or what is good, we are already loading the responses (for each S) with an inbuilt demand for a certain mode of reasoning. Now it might be thought that this hardly matters, that we are eliciting his mode or style of moral reasoning anyway—and if philosophers choose to describe this as 'finding out what Ses mean by moral language', who cares? But this will not do; for there is no necessary connection between what any S means by (say) 'ought' and 'right', on the one hand, and what S's own moral values actually are on the other. To take an extreme case: a teenage S might give very satisfactory answers to questions about what was 'right' or what 'ought to be done', in terms of the reasons given by adults at stages 5 or 6; but, on further investigation, this may only mean that he is good at playing this particular language-game on demand. 'Ought' and 'right' for him mean 'what sophisticated adults tell me'; he does not himself *value* those reasons, and his own moral judgements may be expressed in quite different language—what is 'with it', or 'trendy', or 'groovy', or whatever current slang may be.

This last point, like the others, stems partly from the restricted picture of morality we have been criticising, but it applies more generally. To enlarge on it, we may consider research which seems *prima facie* to fit a wider picture of morality. Williams[1] used interviews to classify children's 'moral thinking', without overtly loading the dice in favour of a particular kind of morality or a particular content; for much of the interview the child was allowed to respond freely to what he thought 'good', 'bad', 'right', or 'wrong', and asked to say why he thought this. The responses of the children were then classified under a number of 'modes of thought' (originally more than ten).

Roughly, then, when the child or interviewer has given an example of something 'wrong' or 'bad', the child is asked 'Why is that wrong (bad)?', and says 'Because . . .'. Now what ambiguities are there here? First, there are at least five things the child may understand by 'wrong'. He may understand (i) what *other people think or say* is wrong or ought not to be done; (ii) what *other people actually avoid doing;* (iii) what *he thinks* (in a general way) is wrong or ought not to be done; (iv) what *he* actually avoids doing; (v) what he thinks *he himself ought* not to do. (If we wanted to, we could make more distinctions still: for instance, we have not considered S's

1. Williams (1969, 1970).

*feelings* about rightness and wrongness, which are distinguishable both from S's *beliefs* and S's *actions*.)

Secondly, when the child says 'Because . . .' he appears to be proffering a reason, but the child may think that the 'reason' is (be proffering it *as*):

(a) a *good* reason, or just *a* (possibly bad) reason.
(b) a reason which is 'ultimate' (stands on its own feet), or which assumes a background of higher-level reasons.
(c) a reason which he would use (have in mind) when acting, or which he knows of but would not use.
(d) a reason which would be also the cause of his behaviour and which he approves of, or a reason which would cause his behaviour and which he does *not* approve of (a reason or cause which, in some sense, operates against his better judgement).

This last possibility (d) reminds us that we have at least to draw some distinction between 'reasons' and 'causes': more precisely, between responses which are meant as *justifications* and those meant only to *explain*. Of course these interconnect in complicated ways; but many responses do not, *prima facie*, even look like reasons in the sense of attempts to justify. They look more like admissions of psychological compulsion, descriptions of emotion or feeling-states, or attempts to render intelligible the kind of 'pulls' which an S is moved by. These differences connect, obviously enough, with different senses or implications that words like 'wrong', 'ought', etc. may have for different Ses. The position is further complicated by the fact that different 'pulls' or syllogisms may operate at different levels of S's mind. One 'part' of S, we may be tempted to say, pulls one way, and another 'part' pulls another: at a given time S may express one 'pull' in his response, at another time another 'pull', and at a third time he may stand back from both 'pulls' and (in some sense) adjudicate between them.

To appreciate these (elementary) distinctions is to gain a distant view of the extent of our own ignorance. Pursuing the linguistic points a little further, we can see the need for listing a number of possible words and phrases which may figure in our questions, along these lines:

Would it be *wrong/right* to . . .?
What *ought you/he/one* to . . .?
What *should you/he/one* . . .?
Would it be *good* (bad, better, worse, best, worst) to . . .?
What *is he to* . . .?

Would it be *mistaken/correct* to . . .?
What is your *duty* . . .?
What are you *obliged* to . . .?

and many other such. These variations are not trivial, insofar as
it *may* be the case that different words and phrases generate or
induce different answers.[1] Are we even clear ourselves about the
conceptual/linguistic differences in 'normal' English usage—let
alone the differences that affect the responses of children and
adolescents?

Nor is this all; for (as always in philosophy) we are concerned
with English usage only in order to establish conceptual, language-
free distinctions, and we cannot be certain that these and other
particular English phrases give us all the differences that are
possible, and hence that are possibly in the minds of our respon-
dents. What responses would we get if we asked French-speaking
children 'Que faut-il faire?', 'Que devez-vous . . .?' or 'Que
devriez-vous . . .?' What distinctions are incorporated in the
German modal verbs—'sollen', 'müssen', etc.? In the Latin 'decet'
or 'oportet', as against 'debeo'? The point here is not that, as good
internationalists, we are concerned with other people besides the
Anglo-Saxon races; the point is that we cannot even begin to
evaluate a 'response' unless we are absolutely clear what the
respondent means, and that this is a long and difficult business.

In this light, even the research-title of 'moral judgement' seems
questionable. By what right do we describe all the responses that
we get from children (or indeed adults) as *judgements?* Many
expressions or sentences could not properly be called judgements
or beliefs at all. It is obvious, for instance, that if I respond to talk
of homosexuality or pork-eating by saying 'Ugh! How foul!', or
something of that kind, I have not necessarily made a judgement
at all: I may have merely expressed my feelings. Further, the
linguistic form may mislead here: although, when doing philosophy,
we can distinguish between 'It's disgusting' and 'It disgusts me',
or between 'It's right' and 'I like it', many people may mean the one
when they say the other.

---

1. Indeed it certainly is the case. In some (non-quantified and unpublished)
research with groups of adolescents, during the process of test-development,
I obtained different answers to the same questions, using the variables 'What
ought you to . . .?' and 'What should you . . .?': and different answers again
with the variables 'What would it be right to . . .?' and 'What would it be good
to . . .?'. I do not need to elaborate this, since the main point is not dependent on
specific research-findings.

It seems plain that many linguistic expressions, particularly in the areas of morality and religion, do not represent beliefs at all, or, at least, they do not represent supposed *truths* to which the speaker is wedded (or even thinks that he is wedded) via the *evidence*. They represent, rather, feelings or fantasies or pictures of some kind to which the speaker is indeed firmly wedded; but it is some emotion that has made the marriage, not any consideration of evidence. When we consider such notions as 'taboo', 'dislike', 'disapproval', 'guilt', 'ego-ideal', 'shame' and many others it is clear that many responses are not judgements at all, although the linguistic forms (usually forced on Ses in test-stories or interviews) may appear in the indicative mood. We cannot tell without further investigation. One Jew may say 'It's wrong to eat pork' and mean that to eat pork is, in fact, a moral mistake, incorrect, unreasonable in terms of whatever reasons he may have in mind; another may say just the same, but mean no more than 'Ugh!' or 'Not for me!'

On the other hand, if we are at all interested in what might generally be called S's moral *commitments*, then it is fairly clear that we cannot satisfactorily determine these without adequate data about S's feelings and *behaviour*. For we should then be interested in those senses of S's response-words ('wrong', 'ought', etc.), or those speech-acts of S, which involved some tendency or commitment to *action* on S's part; and we should not accept the words or speech-acts as sincere, fully 'meant', or whole-hearted unless, in fact, S did characteristically take such action, or take it 'under normal circumstances' (however this phrase be construed). To use a philosopher's term (explained more fully later, p. 30 ff.), we should not know whether S's judgements of certain things as 'right', 'wrong', etc. were genuinely *prescriptive*, unless we had checked these judgements against S's behaviour.

These problems stem not only from the ill-conceived definition of morality in terms of a particular content: that is, so to speak, merely a symptom of the disease. The disease is a *simpliste* view of 'moral' judgement; as we shall see in the next section, 'moral behaviour' is characteristically treated in an equally naive way—indeed, the simple-minded distinction between 'thought' and 'behaviour' in this field just will not do. We are inevitably involved here in a whole range of phenomena which are conceptually distinct. Because of these difficulties, it is not surprising (though it is still regrettable) that researchers have lumped many of them together under such headings as the 'basis', 'style' or 'mode' of moral thinking or behaviour, the 'stage of development', 'character-types' and so on.

What we have here, in fact, is a kind of simple-minded taxonomizing or attempt at classification or at typology. But, on any account, typologies are useless unless there are absolutely clear criteria for assigning people (or whole cultures) to one or the other type. Many modern typologies remind one that we have hardly (if at all) got beyond the stage of typology with which we are familiar from Aristotle's *Nicomachean Ethics* or Theophrastus' *Characters* ('the high-minded man', 'the irascible man', etc.) or from mediaeval medicine ('the bilious' or 'the splenetic man'). These examples in turn remind us of a simple distinction in terms of (a) *description* (usually of dispositions, e.g. 'irascible'), and (b) *cause* (e.g. 'excess of bile'). Even this distinction is not clearly maintained by researchers: for instance, one is often uncertain whether certain terms current in 'mental health' research—'neurotic', 'psychotic', 'schizophrenic'—come under (a) or (b) or under some quite different criteria.

Any typologizing must start from clear descriptions with clear criteria. Many, perhaps all, descriptions may be to some extent 'theory-laden': we may group phenomena together, or separate them, under the influence of some theory or the pressure of a particular purpose. The important thing is to be sure that the descriptions are all of the same *sort*. Thus, to instance a typology at random,[1] one might list five 'types' as follows:

1. Amoral
2. Authoritarian
3. Aggressive
4. Peer-group
5. Mature

There are more cross-categorizations here than are worth our while to analyse: 'authoritarian' seems to refer to S's attitude to authority, 'aggressive' to the kind of emotions S has, 'peer-group' to the sources of influence on S and 'mature' to the author's own preferences. (Worse, these are supposed to be 'developmental stages'.)

Much Piaget-type research seems in fact to consist of attempts at taxonomy or typology of this kind; and the difficulty is always to know what the criteria of classification actually are. Researchers talk of the 'basis', 'modes', 'styles', etc., but none of this is at all clear, as will be seen if we make a few obvious distinctions thus: First, one may choose to categorize children according to their judgements about *what sorts of things* are good or bad, right or

1. (Fortunately) unpublished.

wrong, either (a) if *they* did them, or (b) if *other people* did them. Secondly, one may categorize the *given reasons* of children (see above, p. 17). Thirdly, one may list the children's *general attitude* to certain rules, principles or actions (e.g. whether the child regards them as 'sacred' and unbreakable, or as alterable by mutual consent). Fourthly, one may classify children by *what they regard as the power-source* of the rules (authority, peers, God, etc.): this is to be distinguished from the children's given reasons. Fifthly, there are the *actual influences* on children's morality (parents, peers, etc.). There are no doubt further distinctions to be made.

All these problems (and more) arise when we confront this area. It is no particular discredit to Kohlberg or other workers that they have failed to solve them, but at least they must be confronted. For research into *human* thought and action, whether in morality or other fields, involves a whole new dimension: a dimension in which *reasons, language, intentions, descriptions* and all the apparatus of rationality is of paramount importance. The particular criticisms I have made here are typical of what philosophers would say[1] about much psychological research in general; and it is plausible to say that without a good deal of preliminary work which might be described as descriptive linguistic anthropology, or phenomenology, the kind of experimental results produced even by psychologists of the 'cognitive' school are not likely to stand up to criticism. We shall see in Part II just how difficult this preliminary work is, and what sort of techniques and assessment-methods it requires.

---

1. See PER, and Harré and Secord (1972).

# 3. Problems of assessment: 'affective'

I do not wish the reader to gain the impression that it is conceptual naivety about the notion of 'morality' in particular, or even 'moral judgements', which has generated these difficulties. Essentially the same points crop up in almost all psychological research in this area, under headings like 'temptation-resistance', 'conscience', 'altruism', 'helping behaviour' and so forth. This is no place to attempt a summary of such research,[1] and this would in any case be unnecessary, since the same conceptual considerations apply throughout. But it may be helpful to take a look at one 'affective' or 'motivational' area which has received some attention from competent psychologists under the heading of 'altruism'.

In a recent work entitled *Altruism and Helping Behaviour*[2] the editors confront what they call the 'definitional problems' in a way which suggests at least the glimmerings of conceptual interest and competence. Under the heading 'What is altruism?' they write: 'What is "altruism"?' For Darley and Latane (contributors to a later article in the volume), the researchable question really is 'What determines, in a particular situation, whether or not one person helps another in distress?' By implication in this definition, any behaviour which benefits another in need, regardless of the helper's motives, is altruistic. A very different kind of answer to this question is given by Aronfreed (another contributor). He identifies a basic motive for altruism and confines usage of the term to behaviour which meets this motivational standard. For Aronfreed, altruism is a dispositional component (not a specific form) of behaviour which is controlled by anticipation of its consequences for another individual. He regards empathy as essential for altruism. Unless the actor responds empathetically to social cues conveying another's experience (or to cognitive representation of another's experience), the behaviour cannot be called altruistic. External outcomes to the actor are irrelevant, according to this definition.

1. The best summary is Wright (1971).
2. Macaulay and Berkowitz (1970), pp. 2–3.

Behaviour controlled by expectation of increased self-esteem is also said to be nonaltruistic. The actor must experience empathic or vicarious pleasure, or relief of distress, as a result of behaving in a way that has consequences for another.

'Whether or not empathy is essential to altruism is probably a definitional matter which the reader will have to decide for himself. However, Aronfreed makes a valuable point in questioning very broad usages of the term "altruism". Many different motives may impel one individual to benefit another. Helpful behaviour may stem from social pressures or expectations that all costs will be repaid, perhaps with interest, one way or another. It would be stretching the common meaning of altruism to include such acts.' Later, however, 'We prefer to define altruism more generally, as behaviour carried out to benefit another without anticipation of rewards from external sources. This definition is similar to Rosenhan's "socially autonomous altruism".'

We may remember from elsewhere[1] the connection between human *behaviour* and *intentions,* brought out by Aristotle's remarks,[2] 'Virtuous actions are not done in a virtuous—a just or temperate—way merely because *they* have the appropriate quality. The *doer* must be in a certain frame of mind when he does them. . . . Actions, to be sure, are *called* just and temperate when they are such as a just or temperate man would do. But the doer is just or temperate not because he does such things but when he does them in the way of just and temperate persons'. But the question of *what sort* of reasons or intentions are implied by a description of behaviour is far more open. For instance, supposing I have a rich aunt whom I want to kill. She has a headache; I intend to kill her by bringing her arsenic, but I get the wrong bottle and give her aspirin powder instead. Is this a case where 'one person helps another in distress?' Are we to say that I have helped her, because in fact what I do brings benefit to her (cures the headache), or are we to say that we cannot fairly describe what I did as 'helping', because my intention was not to benefit but to kill her?

Here it is important for the researcher to realize that it does not matter so much what we say, but that it does matter very much whether we are clear about what we mean. If (a) I research into 'helping behaviour', meaning by this *only* behaviour which, in fact, and quite irrespective of what sort of intention the person has, benefits another (as I benefit my aunt), then this is one thing;

---

1. IME, p. 45 ff.
2. *Nicomachean Ethics* (Penguin Translation), pp. 61–2.

if (b) I research into 'helping behaviour', meaning by this *only* behaviour intended by the agent to benefit another, then that is another thing; if (c) I research into 'helping behaviour', meaning by this only behaviour that *both* benefits *and* is intended to benefit, then that is a third thing. Each of (a), (b) and (c) is perfectly legitimate and (in the authors' words) 'researchable'. But they are very different and require different techniques.

Unfortunately much of the passage quoted above introduces a common confusion which diminishes the chances of clarity. First, we are given a summary of Aronfreed's conception—'a dispositional component (not a specific form) of behaviour which is controlled by anticipation of its consequences for another individual'—which looks like quite a reasonable definition of 'altruism'. Making allowance for a penchant for the polysyllabic, we might take this as meaning 'being disposed to act in others' interests', or 'being concerned for the good of others'. But this is immediately followed by 'He regards empathy as essential for altruism'. Now does this mean (1) that part of what is *meant* by 'altruism' is 'empathy', a conceptual or logical connection; or (2) that the behaviour which we call 'altruism' cannot *in practice exist* without empathy, an empirical connection? Certainly some of the following phrases suggest (1): 'the behaviour cannot be *called* altruistic', 'according to this definition', 'stretching the common meaning', etc. If so, we are puzzled about 'empathy', for we would often be prepared to call someone's behaviour 'altruistic' whether or not he had 'empathy': that is, even if he disliked the person he was helping. or even if he did not know the person at all—perhaps indeed particularly in such cases.

However, it may be that Aronfreed uses 'empathy' in such a way that it is a logical or 'definitional' truth that altruism implies empathy. It is in fact very difficult to know whether he does this or not. He wishes to argue 'that the inference of empathic or vicarious mediation of affectivity is the central criterion for the identification of altruism and sympathy', and continues a few lines later '. . . the fact that an act has no directly rewarding external consequences for the actor does not imply that the act functions entirely without reinforcing consequences. From the point of view of the requirements for a more general conception of internalized control of behaviour, we would do better to assume that altruistic acts are indeed governed by the affective value of their anticipation outcomes, and that they often do have reinforcing consequences for the person who carries them out. Even when an altruistic act may have a directly experienced aversive outcome for the actor, the value of its total set of outcomes can nevertheless be preferred to the value of the outcomes of another less altruistic alternative'.[1]

Fighting our way through the jargon, we might come to the conclusion that Aronfreed is going to count *any* process which results in a person's behaving altruistically (i.e. his behaviour being controlled by the anticipation of its consequences for another individual) as some form of 'empathy'. The 'directly experienced outcome' may be 'aversive' (in English, he may not enjoy doing it): but, nevertheless, 'the value of its total set of outcomes can be preferred' (he may still choose or have reason to do it). If he does, in what sense 'must' empathy be at work? Aronfreed might say:

(1) If X cares enough for Y to act in Y's interests, then it is a conceptual truth that empathy must be at work, for by 'empathy' I mean only 'whatever process is involved in caring for Y'.

(2) If X cares enough for Y to act in Y's interests, then it is an empirical or factual truth that empathy—defined independently—is always involved.

'The concept of empathy', he says, 'is tied to observations which allow the inference that a person's affectivity is elicited by the observation (or cognitive representation) of social cues which transmit another person's *experience*.'[2]

This leaves us still in the dark. Suppose (a) I am told that if I give £1 to some society I can help an unknown Indian child. I have no particular feelings about Indian children, but I believe I ought to help other people, so I give the £1. Suppose (b) I hate Smith and want him to suffer, but my father makes me behave nicely to Smith, thus ensuring that my behaviour is 'controlled by the anticipation of its consequences' for Smith—I know that if the consequences aren't nice for Smith, father will punish me. Does (a) or (b), or both or neither, 'allow the inference' that my 'affectivity is elicited', etc.? Both, if this just means that I have got to act in another's interest as a result of *some* motive ('social cues', 'reinforcement', etc.), neither, if it means that only certain processes count—for instance, my feeling pleasure at Smith's smiling face counts, but my fear of being punished by my father or my sternly Kantian adherence to duty doesn't count. The rest of Aronfreed's paper does not make it clear (to me, at least) which alternative he opts for.

I have gone into this example at some length, chiefly in order to

---

1. Macaulay and Berkowitz (1970), pp. 104–5.
2. ibid., p. 107 (his italics).

bring out the dangers of muddle *at the first stage* of research. Psychologists would do better either to tackle this stage properly, or else to leave it strictly alone and simply demonstrate empirical co-variances. I have much sympathy with Aronfreed's general drift, but, in a way, his occasional flirting with conceptual points just makes things worse. He half grasps the (important if obvious) conceptual point that such terms as 'altruism', 'concern', etc. normally imply that X acts for a certain reason, namely that his action will be governed by the criterion of Y's interests—that not just *any* 'helpful behaviour' normally counts as altruistic. We then expect, from a psychologist, some facts concerning what predisposes or causes X to use such a reason. *One* general cause or process, 'empathy', is held out to us, but it is heavily disguised as *the* (only?) cause or process that could (logically?) produce altruism.

To do better, we would have to start by a clearer analysis of 'altruism', 'concern', etc. In any sense of these terms which is relevant to education, the first thing to notice is the importance of the *description under which* the agent sees his action. If I am a ruthless estate-owner, like the elder Cato, I may be 'concerned with', or 'care for', my slaves because they are valuable property. These slaves are also, at least in our eyes, 'other people'. So there is a sense in which we can say that I am 'caring for other people' or have 'concern for others'. But we here use our description, not Cato's. Cato's concern is not for people as such, but for people as property. Similarly, the point of the parable of the Good Samaritan is to bring out the importance of using the general description 'person' or 'person in need' as the starting-point for one's behaviour, and not particular descriptions such as 'Jew', 'Levite', 'Samaritan', etc. We cannot say whether a person is concerned with other people as such unless and until we know what description he is using.

We may put essentially the same point by demonstrating the importance of the *reason* for a person's behaviour, of *why* he acts or fails to act. If I behave nicely (considerately, helpfully, etc.) to my subordinates or superiors, to attractive blondes or flattering friends, to rich aunts or dangerous criminals, it is (here obviously) an open question whether I am responding to them as to people *qua* people on the one hand, or, on the other hand, to them as entities that I see as useful to me, sexual objects, rich, flattering, dangerous, etc. I may use either of two basic kinds of reasons, which go along with the two kinds of descriptions: either of the form 'Because this is another person with needs and wants like me', or of the form 'Because he's rich' (powerful, dangerous, useful, etc.).

To say this is not to say that the person who is genuinely concerned for people as such must be able to enunciate this reason fluently, or give any kind of philosophical account of its validity. But it is to say that *this must be* his reason (and description), not something else. Normally we would determine this in the way that we usually determine such things, namely by *asking* the person. Of course, it would be possible to make a fair guess by observing a sufficient number of instances of behaviour. Suppose, for example, that we had an allegedly virtuous and simple-minded peasant who could give no account at all of why he acted as he did (though such a person would have to be unbelievably simple-minded). We see that he behaves considerately to his fellow-villagers; but, of course, we are not sure whether this is because they are fellow-villagers or because they are people. S we test him out by introducing him to people of a different colour, religion, language, manners, morals, etc. If he still acts considerately, we are part of the way towards fairly claiming that it is people *qua* people that he uses as a reason, not some other description.

Cases of inconsiderate or unconcerned behaviour are equally open to ambiguity. A person may be said to 'hate Pakistanis' (Jews, teachers, the police, etc.), but this does not necessarily mean that he hates them under that description—he may not even know what a Pakistani *is*. Under what description, then, does he hate these entities? *Qua* aliens (threats, authorities, etc.)? And what counts as 'alien' *to him?* Colour? Accent? Religion? Manners? In order to understand the person's behaviour—the syllogism he was following in acting—we should have to consider all this. Plainly if we wish to teach or engender concern we need to know what counter-syllogisms are likely to operate.

In order for a person to 'behave altruistically', 'have concern', or 'care' for others, the following seem to be logically required:

(a) He must have the concept of a person (know what a person is), otherwise he cannot use the requisite description and reason for action. Actually, a firm and clear grasp of this concept is not common even amongst adults.

(b) He must, 'in theory' at least, claim to use (think he ought to use) this concept (description), as against other concepts, as his overriding reason for acting. That is, he must believe that 'because he's a person' ought to take precedence over, e.g. 'because he's an alien', 'because he's my enemy', etc.

(c) He must have some kind of *feeling* attached to this concept as a principle of action. That is, he must have some interest invested in the idea of something's 'being a person'. This is to be contrasted with various feelings, affections, sentiments, etc. which are (as it were, accidentally) directed towards people, but not towards people as such (e.g. towards attractive blondes, 'appealing' infants, etc.).

(d) His claim to the principle based on the concept (b), and his feelings attached to it (c), must override other syllogisms in practice, so that he actually makes a decision to *act* in a considerate way.

(e) He must in fact act in this way (unless prevented).

I think that all these are distinct [though (d) and (e) might be merged[1]]. Later[2] I have described them under the shorthand of PHIL(HC), PHIL(CC), PHIL(RSF), KRAT(1) and KRAT(2).

It is at once evident that most, perhaps all, tests or assessments used by experimental psychologists fail to clarify which of (a)–(e) above the test-results tell us. I shall not describe any of these assessments at length here, but the usual reason for failure is that simple and *single* observations or responses are thought to be sufficient (almost as if one could classify a piece of behaviour as 'altruistic' without worrying about the descriptions or reasons of the agent at all; part of the trouble here is the belief in 'motivation' as something logically separable from human action). Some tests, like Kohlberg's or the Warborough PHIL/DIK tests,[3] give some indication of PHIL(CC); but that is about all.

Now that the complexities are somewhat clearer, we may well begin to feel dissatisfied with the 'cognitive-affective' distinction in general. We are accustomed to this distinction in fairly sharp terms, not only in psychological research but also in much philosophy and common-sense moralizing in our culture: (i) knowing what one ought to do, and (ii) doing it. But even a naive phenomenological consideration gives us cause for dissatisfaction. Consider the very common case where a person *misdescribes* the situation before him. As a thug in London, he sees a person and calls him 'bloody Pakistani', and beats him up; as a Roman governor or Pharisee, he sees the innocent Jesus and calls him 'a troublemaker' or 'a blasphemer', and sentences him to death. Are we to call this a 'cognitive' or an 'affective' ('motivational') failure? As some philosophers [see in particular Murdoch (1970)] have stressed, a person's moral behaviour will depend very much on how he has furnished the world he lives in: on his conceptual apparatus, and

1. ERE, p. 144 ff.
2. Part II, pp. 38–9.
3. See under 'Further reading'.

the use he makes of it. S1 sees Jews or Pakistanis as alien, hostile, threatening; S2 sees anyone who challenges the established régime as a 'trouble-maker'.

Naturally we could argue about these and other cases at length, but even this brief mention of them should show that we need much more phenomenological caution. Unless we attend to the facts, any description may mislead: 'lack of motivation', 'weakness of will', 'not caring', 'akrasia', or any other. Significantly, we often forget that this problem arises not only, nor even peculiarly, in the 'moral' sphere (as culturally defined), but in any case of practical human action. We need to know what is going on in the mind of the child who does not do his Latin sentences properly, just as in the mind of the child who does not behave well towards other people. In many of these cases, the cognitive-affective distinction is difficult or impossible to follow through.

This reminds us only of what we know quite well already:[1] that the 'motivation' of particular pieces of 'behaviour' is unintelligible apart from S's 'cognitive' processes; and, more important here, that the 'cognitive' processes are unintelligible except by reference to the conceptual world in which S is living at the time. To enlarge briefly: If we wanted to know what a chess-playing S's 'motivation' was for playing P-Q4, we could not determine this without determining his 'cognitive' reasons (which, given the background of his wanting to win the game, are unintelligible unless seen in relation to the rules and principles of chess-playing and to S's perception of these rules and principles).

Now there are dissimilarities between various moral systems, on the one hand, and games, on the other: notably, that most adult human beings adhere more consciously and consistently to the rules of games than to moral systems. There are also, however, important similarities. Both are rule-governed structures, and the 'motivation' of an S already operating within such a structure is to be conceived quite differently from that of an S who is not. In other words, we are not dealing with isolated pieces of 'altruism' or 'concern' or 'helping behaviour', any more than we would be dealing with the isolated pushing of a piece of wood (a pawn) two squares forwards (P-Q4). Almost everything will depend on how S sees the situation; in an important sense, it will often be true that the 'motivation' *comes with the concepts*. That is why researchers need a much more sophisticated phenomenological break-down.

---

1. PER, section 9.

# 4. First steps towards assessment

Assessment follows from definition; and if (as I have argued) we are to seek a logical rather than an empirical criterion of what is to count as 'morality', and one which is genuinely content-free, then it seems wisest to follow the prescriptivist philosophers (notably Hare)[1] and work in terms of prescriptiveness, overridingness and universalization.

These (perhaps somewhat daunting) terms can be simplified without too much loss. We are to be concerned with the most important principles that govern what a person does and feels. Human action and feeling is characteristically rule-governed: that is, people do and feel things *for certain reasons*, or in accordance with certain principles. I do not mean that their behaviour is *caused*. Twitches, knee-jerks, and other involuntary pieces of human behaviour are caused, but they are not rule-governed—they are not things that people *do*, but rather things that *happen* to them. I mean that their actions and emotions are (characteristically) to be seen as following from something like a syllogism or argument.

Aristotle's 'practical syllogism' is the earliest (and perhaps still the best) model for this. A man wants something, or thinks it desirable, or accepts that he ought or ought not to do something; for instance, he may accept the principle that one ought to help other people in need. He then comes across a case that falls under the principle—say, somebody who is hungry or in pain. Then, as the 'conclusion' of the 'argument', he helps him. Of course we do not always, perhaps not even often, go through all these steps in conscious ratiocination. But that, nevertheless, is how we think and act. We act for reasons: that is, we say to ourselves (or could say if asked) something like 'I did that *because* it falls under a particular principle' or 'because it serves some end' ('I braked because I wanted to avoid an accident', or 'I fed him because he was hungry and in need, and I think one ought to help people in need').

1. Hare (1952, 1963).

All such arguments are 'practical' or 'prescriptive' if they characteristically issue in action. I mean simply that the rules and principles are not just inert: in adopting them we thereby commit ourselves to action, or (as it were) order ourselves to act. We are not just describing what other people want or think good; we are prescribing certain kinds of action for ourselves to perform. But only some of them are 'overriding'. This is a matter of which principles win when a conflict arises. We may guess from Nero's fiddling while Rome burned that some principle like 'Practise the violin' or 'Have a good time' overrode principles like 'Save human life' or 'Emperors ought to take charge in crises'.

Again, only some principles are 'universalized'. What I want or like is one thing: but what I think is *right* or *good*, or what I think I *ought* to do, is something else. In the latter case—although not necessarily in these words—I claim something as a rule for *everybody*, or at least everybody in a relevantly similar situation. This is not a question of what sort of reasons I have; I might, for instance think that I (one, anyone) ought not to steal because the authorities will probably catch and punish me (one). This is a 'universalized' judgement all right. The difference is between saying this sort of thing and saying something like 'I happen not to want to be caught and punished by the authorities, so I'd better not steal'—perhaps adding 'but you chaps may have quite different desires; I'm not laying down any rules for anyone else'. It is important for researchers to note (as we have seen) that the difference here need not lie in the actual *words* ('ought', 'good', etc.) but in the sort of claim that is being made. Either I am just talking about my own personal desires and how to fulfil them, or else I am making some public, 'universalized' claim about what is good or right for *anyone* in a similar situation, irrespective of what he may personally desire.

All this has been more fully explained elsewhere[1] and need not be elaborated here. We propose, then, to define a person's morality— his moral judgements, principles, actions and feelings—by the criterion of what he commits himself to (prescriptive), what is of central importance to him (overriding), and what he thinks applies to all other people in a relevantly similar situation (universal). It will be clear, when we remember the 'practical syllogism', that this definition may include many things that particular social groups do not count as 'moral'. For it is anybody's guess just what *are* people's overriding principles of action: they may be far re-moved from anything to do with basic 'social morality', and still

---

1. See particularly Hare (1963).

farther removed from the particular conventional codes or 'moralities' of various social groups.

There are various reasons (apart from those already given)
why such a definition seems sensible for the researcher. The
chief of these is the connection between morality and actual
*behaviour and feeling.* This comes out most obviously if we are
interested in education: if education in morality is to be of
much use, it must concern itself with a concept of morality
which is tightly tied to what people actually *do.* To educate
people in non-prescriptive morality—that is, in a set of conventions or principles to which they themselves may attach no
weight or commitment—is, in effect, not to educate them *in*
morality at all: it is just to inform them about other people's
morality.[1]

But the point has force for any researcher in the field. For the
mere existence of moral rules and principles 'on paper' (so to speak),
or in public ritual pronouncements, may tell us little about the
actual intentions, motives and rule-governed behaviour of people.
We need to know what they do and why, not just how they relate
to some particular moral code or content—which may, indeed,
play a very small part in their lives. In the same way, if we were
interested in the actual religious feelings and behaviour of people,
we should not necessarily capture much of this just by observing
whether they had their children baptized in church, or put down
'Church of England' on official forms. We should need a criterion
for 'religious' which related more closely to their own inner feelings
and principles of action.

So far as the more constructive part of this book is concerned
(Part II), I shall be relying upon the picture here painted, in terms
of a man's overriding principles. A full account of what this means
for research is given in Part II. Some readers may find this picture
easier to understand if it is entitled not 'morality' but something
like 'practical action', or 'one's most important principles of
behaviour'. Of course this is a very large area for research; too
large, some might think, to be dealt with *en masse.* It would perhaps
be possible, after a good deal more hard philosophical thinking,
to break down the area into a number of sub-areas: for instance,
as I have suggested elsewhere,[2] into 'interpersonal morality' (where
others' interests are at stake), 'prudential morality' or 'ideals'
(where they are not), and 'mental health' cases, where no question

1. Cf. ERE, pp. 8–9.
2. IME, Ch. 2.

of *interests* or practical action arises, but where nevertheless we may still want to speak of 'moral' deficiency in some sense of the word. Other break-downs would also be possible, e.g. between 'social morality', on the one hand, and 'ideals', on the other, or between sub-areas where uniquely 'moral blame' or 'moral praise' is applicable (if we can make sense of these difficult notions) and sub-areas where it is not. It seems to me, however, that there are good reasons for avoiding break-downs of this kind, for purposes of empirical research. There is another way by which we may tackle the area piece-meal, as of course we must do; but I must defer explanation of this until Part II, when we deal with the 'moral components'.

This does not, of course, imply that the work of other researchers in the past and present is in any simple sense 'wrong', nor even that they have used a 'wrong definition' of morality: still less that their empirical findings are unimportant. It implies, I think, two things. First, because of the lack of clarity in definition (and hence in assessment-procedures), it is simply not clear *just what the 'findings' actually show*. Secondly, future research would do well to *begin* by a close consideration of these and other logical or philosophical points, rather than charge too quickly into more empirical considerations of measurement, scoring of tests, factor analysis, and so on.

I now want to put together some of the points made hitherto, to see if we can sketch out a fuller and more coherent picture of how to assess 'moral thinking' and 'moral behaviour'.

1. I have throughout stressed, and want to re-emphasize here, that in attempting to assess human (rational) behaviour we have to assess S's *reasons*, and the *rules* or principles S follows when he performs the action. This cannot be done merely by observing overt physical movements—by just taking photographs, as it were. We have to know 'what goes on in S's head', what 'overriding syllogism' S is following at the time. It may seem that the researcher can easily guess (induce) this from S's overt behaviour; and under certain conditions this may be true. But these conditions are not easy to establish, and, in any case, we should certainly require cross-checks in the standard form of verification for human reasons and intentions—namely, by *asking* S what his reasons and intentions were. This method of verification raises important problems of sincerity and rationalization, which we shall deal with later.[1] But we cannot do without it.

1. p. 73 ff.

This point cuts deeper than might be supposed and I shall reinforce it by three examples used elsewhere:[1]

(a) Suppose we are trying to assess various Ses for generosity. We observe them passing by a beggar, in turn. Each puts his hand in his pocket and gives the beggar £1. S1, however, does this because he is sorry for the beggar; S2 because he wants to show off to his girl friend; S3 because he thinks this will gain him a reward in the next world; S4 to get rid of his guilt-feelings; and so on. We can, if we like, say that their behaviour or actions were generous; but obviously they are not, in any serious sense, equally generous people, for they are following different rules and syllogisms.

(b) Suppose now that we are trying to assess Ses for 'honesty', and put them in situations where they can cheat. S1 cheats because he doesn't see anything wrong with cheating anyway; S2 cheats to gain an advantage; S3 cheats because he wants to disobey the authorities (when he can get away with it); S4 does not cheat, because there is someone around (even if not watching) who makes him feel guilty about it; S5 does not cheat, because he is the son of a gentleman, and 'gentlemen's sons don't cheat', except in some circumstances; S6 does not cheat, because it seems to him more fun to abide by the rules; and so on. Now we can say that S1–3 cheated, and S4–6 did not cheat, but (without further verification) that is *all* we can say, and it is not much if we are really interested in *honesty*.

(c) Suppose we are assessing S for his tendency to kill. Concealed in bushes with telescopes, we discover that S kills foxes, single individuals with pistols whom he meets at dawn, and foreigners— sometimes on alien soil, sometimes in his own country. 'This is "situation-specific" ', we conclude. So far as *killing* is concerned, so good. But, of course, S is a gentleman who engages in fox-hunting, duelling, and (when honour requires) war. He follows—and follows consistently or 'generally'—an overriding principle, or syllogism of the form 'I ought to act honourably: this is an honourable action: therefore do this'. In the case of this S, he does not do what he regards as 'murder'—which is probably (for him) dishonourable.

2. From this, two points follow. First, if we predefine and thereby limit the area of morality to specific situations (the 'public norms' of honesty, truth-telling, etc.) we shall be apt to overlook different types of reasons. Secondly, unless we find out 'what goes on in S's

1. PER, section 3.

head', we shall be apt to forget the importance of what *concepts* S uses in his behaviour. Thus we may operate with the simple pair 'honesty'/'dishonesty', whereas S is operating with 'honourable'/ 'dishonourable', or some quite different pair. When S meets a situation, S will *see* the situation *as* (describe it to himself as) this or that, and 'this or that' may be almost anything. You call it murder; I call it revenge; Siegfried calls it exercise; Hitler calls it purifying the State; and so on. The description S gives may be caused *by* S's overriding principles, or it may be the cause *of* S's choice of one principle rather than another. (S1, a Pharisee, is on the look-out for trouble-makers, being frightened about his authority, so he identifies Jesus as a trouble-maker rather than under the description of an 'innocent man'. S2, another Pharisee, has it brought to his attention that Jesus is a trouble-maker, and this arouses his fears, sparking off a 'put down trouble-makers' syllogism rather than an 'acquit the innocent' one).

Rather than elaborate these problems, it will be more profitable to try to make a fairly comprehensive list of the different aspects of moral thought and behaviour which any serious assessor must attend to. These 'aspects', 'components' or 'constituents' are not psychological entities, 'factors', 'traits', 'constructs' or anything of that kind. They will be derived, not from any theory or hypothesis about 'mental mechanisms', but simply from a consideration of *what it means* to think and act morally, and from what is necessarily implied by this. I stress this (and shall enlarge on it later),[1] because the whole burden of our criticism is that empirical researchers have been too hasty in their approach; they have not succeeded in bridging the vital gap between what is normally meant by moral thought and action on the one hand, and practical assessment and empirical evidence on the other—partly because they have not realized just how wide the gap is.[2]

---

1. p. 64.
2. Research on animal behaviour may conveniently be mentioned here. Since chimpanzees, dogs, etc. lack language and concepts, words like 'sympathy', 'keeping promises', 'helping other people', etc. will not apply, at least in their normal senses, if at all. Nor can one *educate* (though one may *train*) animals. Nor does the concept of morality apply to them. The use of such research will be to lay bare certain mechanisms, 'imprinted' behaviour-patterns, 'learned responses', etc. which human beings (may) also have. The researcher in morality, and the moral educator, will have to take these into account *not* as part of what is meant by 'morality', but as non-rational features of the human animal which may inhibit or accelerate certain types of 'moral development'. This in no way diminishes their practical importance: but this importance has (logical) limits. See ERE, Ch. 7.

Basically the making of such a list will be no more than an elaboration of those aspects of thought and behaviour which are relevant to S's following an overriding principle or 'practical syllogism'. But there are many such aspects, and the serious researcher ought at least to be interested in the following:

(a)  What concepts S *has* (e.g. of 'other people', 'honour', 'honesty', etc.).

(b)  What concepts S *thinks he ought to use* in his behaviour: that is, what rules or principles he thinks he ought to follow. (I may have the concept of 'honour' without thinking that I ought to use it when deciding how to act.)

(c)  What *feelings* or emotions S has (under normal conditions) that support his belief that he should use these concepts and principles. (I may have the concept of 'honour', think (in a general or theoretical way) that I ought to use it, etc., but have no feelings attached to it—I do not feel remorse when I fail to deploy it, for instance.)

(d)  What knowledge or awareness S has of the surrounding circumstances. This would include:

  (i)  S's ability to identify his own and others' emotions
  (ii)  S's knowledge of the 'hard' facts relevant to what he decides to do.

(e)  What 'know-how' or 'social skills' S has in dealing with people: since much of S's moral behaviour may turn on this.

(f)  Whether S *brings to bear* the above on those situations with which he is actually confronted in 'real life'. This would include:

  (i)  Whether S notices or is alert to the situation, and describes it in a way related to the concepts in (a) and (b) above, or in some other way.
  (ii)  Whether S makes full or partial use of his knowledge and awareness in (d) and (e) above.
  (iii)  Whether S actually *does* use the principles he claims as right ((b) above), supported by his feelings ((c) above), so as to make a sincere *decision* to act in a certain way: or whether he uses other principles.

(g)  Whether S *does* actually act in accordance with his decision.

I think it would be mistaken for any researcher to form *a priori* opinions on the comparative importance of some of these aspects as against others. One reason for this is that they are in an important sense cumulative: thus S has a concept, thinks he ought to use it, feels he ought to use it, has various kinds of knowledge and skill relevant to using it, brings these to bear when facing a 'real life' situation, and acts on this basis. Differences—whether we call them 'successes' or 'failures'—may occur at any point. To ask how 'important' those differences are is already to have adopted some viewpoint about the importance of a certain type of research. Thus if we have already decided to make it our main concern to discover whether S performs certain overt actions (never mind why he does), then we shall be tempted to concentrate on (g): but this would be an error, even in its own terms. For moral thought and action are, as we have tried to show, too intimately connected both logically and empirically to allow of such an approach.

It is at this point that the particular interest of the researcher becomes relevant. As was pointed out in the preface, his interest may lie in the 'non-normative' rather than the 'normative' area. He may be concerned to assess the moral thought and behaviour of various Ses from no special standpoint, but simply to categorize them and account for their differences. Here he might want to make use of some of the typologies mentioned earlier: perhaps to classify those Ses who are 'other-obeying', 'self-obeying', etc. Alternatively, he may take the standpoint of the moral *educator*, in which case he will be interested primarily in how far the morality of various Ses is rational or reasonable: in a 'normative' approach.

The point I want to stress here is that both kinds of researcher need to work from a list of 'aspects', 'components' or 'constituents', of the sort made in 2. above. In the rest of this book we shall be dealing with assessment from the 'normative' researcher's viewpoint. We shall use a list of 'moral components', giving each of these brief titles for conciseness and clarity. But these components will be no more than mentioned in the above list *considered from a 'normative' viewpoint*. For example, (a) and (b) of our list were concerned with whether S had certain concepts, and whether he thought he ought to use them in moral decision and action. Now the 'normative' researcher (for reasons given elsewhere)[1] will think that the concepts S *ought* to have, and ought to think he should use, are concerned with the interests of other people, the equality of 'moral status' among all human beings, and so on. So his concern will be to determine whether S has, and thinks he should use, *these* concepts. The 'non-normative' researcher may not be interested in whether S has these particular concepts. But he must still be interested in what concepts S does have, and thinks he should use.

1. IME, Ch. 4: ERE, Appendix III.

(a) and (b) will still apply, though not necessarily in the form given to them by the 'normative' researcher.

I have argued at length elsewhere[1] (and shall not repeat here) that the 'normative' researcher ought to use something like our set of 'moral components', both on grounds of research-strategy and on more strictly philosophical grounds. Here I want to stress the importance (for both kinds of researcher) of giving these clear titles and definitions. The odd-sounding titles we shall use— PHIL, EMP, GIG and so on—are more than merely convenient. First, they wean us from vague 'global' terms such as 'sensitivity', 'awareness', 'maturity', 'a responsible attitude' and so forth. Secondly, they force us to be clear about their definitions, so that we are sure about what we are trying to assess. Thirdly, they force us to try to cover all the ground—to identify (putting it negatively) what can go wrong with S's moral thought and behaviour, to clarify all the logical types of failure.

I make no apology, then, for asking the reader to familiarize himself with this (simple) terminology; indeed I would warn him against any radically dissimilar approach. I do not claim that the following list, which has been revised and added to from earlier literature, is either at all points complete or at all points conceptually watertight. Much remains to be done, even at the purely conceptual level. But I think it will stand as a sensible basis both for 'normative' and 'non-normative' research, and that it is sufficiently well developed for empirical researchers to use as a framework. I shall explain the logic, status and assessment-methods relevant to each component in following sections: here I shall simply list them, correlating each with the list we have just made for 'non-normative' research.

| | | |
|---|---|---|
| [a][2] | PHIL(HC) | Having the concept of a 'person'. |
| [b] | PHIL(CC) | Claiming to use this concept in an overriding, prescriptive and universalized (O, P and U) principle. |
| [c] | PHIL(RSF)(DO & PO) | Having feelings which support this principle, either of a 'duty-oriented' (DO) or a 'person-oriented' (PO) kind. |
| [d(i)] | EMP(HC) | Having the concepts of various emotions (moods, etc.). |

1. ibid.
2. The letters [a], [b], etc. refer to the earlier list on p. 36.

| [d(i)] | EMP(1)(Cs) | Being able, in practice, to identify emotions, etc. in one-self, when these are at a conscious level. |
| [d(i)] | EMP(1)(Ucs) | Ditto, when the emotions are at an unconscious level. |
| [d(i)] | EMP(2)(Cs) | Ditto, in other people, when at a conscious level. |
| [d(i)] | EMP(2)(Ucs) | Ditto, when at an unconscious level. |
| [d(ii)] | GIG(1)(KF) | Knowing other ('hard') facts relevant to moral decisions. |
| [d(ii)] | GIG(1)(KS) | Knowing sources of facts (where to find out) as above. |
| [e] | GIG(2)(VC) | 'Knowing how'—a 'skill' element in dealing with moral situations, as evinced in verbal communication with others. |
| [e] | GIG(2)(NVC) | Ditto, in non-verbal communication. |
| [f(i)] | KRAT(1)(RA) | Being, in practice, 'relevantly alert' to (noticing) moral situations, and seeing them as such (describing them in terms of PHIL, etc. above). |
| [f(ii)] | KRAT(1)(TT) | Thinking thoroughly about such situations, and bringing to bear whatever PHIL, EMP and GIG one has. |
| [f(iii)] | KRAT(1)(OPU) | As a result of the foregoing, making an overriding, prescriptive and universalized decision to act in others' interests. |
| [g] | KRAT(2) | Being sufficiently whole-hearted, free from unconscious counter-motivation, etc. to carry out (when able) the above decision in practice. |

It will be seen that the 'normative' list is merely a slight extension or sophistication of the 'non-normative' list made earlier, with this difference: we are here concerned with a particular type of morality (roughly, an 'other-considering' type). Hence the technical term PHIL, and the restriction of KRAT to bringing *this* principle (not *any* principle), to bear, making a decision of *this* type, and acting on it.

'Non-normative' researchers, as I have said, must use a list *of this kind*. It would be perfectly practical (and might save trouble) to use the same technical terms, but substituting for PHIL (and altering the definition of KRAT accordingly) the researcher's own interests. For instance, if he were concerned with research into an 'honour' ethic, he could replace PHIL by some other term—perhaps TIM, if we are going to keep to Greek—and see how far various Ses brought their TIM to bear so as to make an overriding decision, and so forth. Or if the researcher wishes to leave it open, having no particular interest in one kind of morality rather than in another, he can use some blanket term for whatever concepts and principles S has, and claims to use, and has feelings about. However, it is not my business to make further suggestions on these points of practical detail.

Two further points must be noted. First, these components are (as we have noticed) *cumulative*. We can represent this in a simplified question:

$$\left.\begin{array}{l} \text{PHIL} \\ \text{EMP} \\ \text{GIG} \end{array}\right\} \text{plus KRAT(1) lead to right decision: right decision plus KRAT(2) lead to right action.}$$

In earlier literature[1] we marked the stage of 'right decision' by one of two other technical terms, DIK and PHRON: DIK where others' interests were concerned, PHRON where they were not. These two terms will not figure largely in what follows.

They introduce a second point, however, which is that this list of components may be used for the assessment of that part of morality which is not, or not centrally, concerned with the interests of other people: in particular, of 'moral ideals', religious and other outlooks, the 'prudence' and 'mental health' cases mentioned elsewhere,[2] and so forth. PHIL, of course, will (by definition) not be relevant here, since others' interests are not at stake. But the list should still be useful for those researchers who do not wish to be confined to the area of inter-personal morality.

Without further ado or explanation, then, we shall take a closer look at these components and how to assess for them. A full understanding of each is essential, and I would ask the reader to go through the following sections with care: for without a firm grasp of the components, the later remarks on assessment-methods and the sketches of assessments will be at best misleading and at worst incomprehensible.

1. IME, Ch. 4.          2. ERE, Ch. 10: IME, Ch. 2.

# Part II

## Assessment

# 5. The moral components

**PHIL**

Under the heading PHIL we have to make sense of the area often described in such terms as 'concern for others', 'sympathy', 'sense of fair play', 'respect for other people', and so forth. As this is one of the most important components, so also it is most liable to confusion and vagueness. We shall try to break it down into a number of logically distinct parts.

### 1. Having the concept of a 'person'

The first thing that seems to be required is that S should have a clear concept of a 'person' or the 'other', in the sense demanded by morality. Briefly, this concept involves a criterion of similarity in virtue of which all 'rational animate creatures' are put into the same category. By 'rational animate creatures', I mean all entities who are (in the full sense) language-users, and to whom we can correctly ascribe such terms as 'will', 'emotion', 'intention', 'purpose' and 'consciousness'. Such creatures will also have wants, needs and desires in a fuller, or at least a different, sense than that in which we may say that plants or machines or animals have wants, needs and desires.[1]

Of course there are both logical and empirical difficulties here. We may be logically uncertain about whether (say) dolphins and chimpanzees are to count as 'rational animate creatures', even if we know all the empirical facts about them: and/or we may be empirically uncertain about the facts—do dolphins really have a language? But the vast majority of cases are clear, and the concept can be established clearly enough to enable us to know, for instance, what sorts of entities discovered on Mars would in principle count as 'people' in the required sense. Similarly we may be doubtful about the age at which infants can be said to count as 'people':

1. PER, section 2.

but at least the concept allows us to dismiss as irrelevant such considerations as sex, skin-colour, race, height, creed, and many others.

It is important that we should remember what is meant by 'having the concept of'. As I use the phrase, it will refer solely to S's ability to conceive of all 'people' as forming one class, and (given the facts) to identify any 'person' as a member of that class. This ability is verified by S's being able to *say*, to himself and in principle to others, something like 'This entity has intentions and needs, uses language, etc., therefore it counts as a person'. S must not merely react or behave differently towards people and non-people, but must do so for a reason—namely, because he sees them as different in terms of this criterion. Nor is there any requirement that S must have an 'image', 'mental picture', 'ideas', 'set' or anything else that suggests the existence of some 'psychological entity' or the working of some 'psychological mechanism'. That way lies confusion.

Equally, 'having the concept of' does not imply either of two things which even philosophers have sometimes seemed to imply. First, it does not imply that S has what I shall call the 'practical' ability to identify cases of the concept. One may have the concept of an alkali without, in laboratory practice, having the ability to identify an alkali; of checkmate, without being very good, over the chess-board, at recognizing cases of checkmate. Suppose that some of the entities on Mars are people, but that in practice it is difficult to distinguish these entities from robots or other non-rational arte-facts. Then S may have the concept of a person so long as he can say '*If* this entity can really talk, feel, intend, etc., then it counts as a person', and he may add 'though without more experience and practice (or sharper eyesight or other "practical" abilities) I find it hard to recognize which entities are of this kind'. Secondly, and more simply (although not less importantly for research), *having* the concept does not entail *using* or wanting to use the concept. I have the concept 'made of wood', but I do not normally see my room as divided between wooden and non-wooden objects. I shall only *use* the concept in certain circumstances, e.g. if I am frightened of woodworm or fire.[1]

In assessing Ses for 'having the concept of a person', shall we allow ourselves to say that an S has 'some of the concept', or 'part of the concept' or 'is on the way towards having the concept'? The answer to this is 'No' to the first two, but 'Yes' to the third.

1. PER, section 7.

Suppose S begins by counting all bipeds, but not one-legged men or rational Martians, as people. Then we try to push him a stage further, and he counts all men but still not Martians. Then, finally, he includes all rational, animate creatures. What we should say here is that, at the first stages, he has *a* concept but it is not *the* concept (the concept we want him to have). 'Person' for him means, first, 'all bipeds', then perhaps 'all men on earth'. It is not till the last stage that he has *the* concept. Before then, he does not in any serious sense have 'part of' it; he just has a different concept. However, if our interests are in the empirical learning-process, and if we have some kind of picture of stages of learning through which S has to go if he is to end up with the concept, we can certainly say such things as 'he is on the way towards getting the concept', or 'he has nearly got it'. But this is a very different matter. In assessing whether someone has the concept or not, we must say 'Either he has it or he hasn't'.

## 2. Claiming the concept as a moral principle

This aspect of PHIL is much more difficult. I have written 'claiming', not 'using' or 'applying', the concept because I want to exclude from this aspect certain things better assessed elsewhere. I want to exclude the question of whether S uses the concept of 'other people's interests' when S is actually faced with the necessity or opportunity for moral decision and action 'in the field': that is, not in any artificial test-situation but in the outside world. S may, or may not, use this as his overriding criterion for *deciding* what to do, and, again, S may or may not feel the criterion as strong, or overriding, enough for S actually to *behave* in accordance with it. Both these are important, but I am not concerned with them here. I am concerned rather with whether S in general—one might say in principle or as part of his moral theory—thinks that this is the criterion which he ought to use, whether S claims it as the sort of reason that ought to influence him.

This does not, however, excuse us from so constructing our assessments that we can be sure that S claims—or, in this very restricted context, 'applies'—this criterion as a genuinely prescriptive, overriding and universal one. It will be best to illustrate this and the preceding points by an example. Suppose we present S with a story describing a situation in which other people's interests are involved, and in which he may use them as a criterion for decision and action. We then ask S what he thinks ought to be done, and we suppose that S says that other people's interests should be satisfied. Then (1) this does not (and is not intended to) tell us whether S *would* in fact use this criterion if he were, in real life, the agent—*either* (a) in his decision-making, *or* (b) in his actual behaviour. All it tells us is that S thinks he ought to use it, that S claims it as his principle. But (2) we need to know more than this: (i) S must mean his 'ought' prescriptively: that is, as *committing* him, S, to action. S must mean something like 'It isn't just that this would be a good thing to do: I think that, in such a situation, *I* ought to commit myself to (order myself, prescribe to myself) such decision and action'. (ii) S must mean his 'ought' overridingly: S must think that this is what he ought to do *more than anything else*. (iii) S must mean his 'ought' universally: S must think that he, *and anyone else* similarly placed, ought to do it.[1]

It is easy to see from this (without going into too much detail) that we have both certain limitations, and certain detailed obligations, for testing in this area. First, we must *avoid* trying to find out what S would in fact ('in the field') decide or do—or, of course, what S thinks anyone else would in fact decide or do. Second, we must *ensure* that we do not rest content with knowing what S thinks some other agent ought to do, or what S thinks that he (S) but not some other agent ought to do, or what S's judgement on actual decisions (given in the story) is, or what S thinks would be 'nice to happen' but not (prescriptively) ought to be done. All these considerations will affect the form of our tests and assessments.

As we have said, we are here concerned with S's beliefs, basic principles or 'moral theory', and to get at this, we have to *exclude* 'in-the-field' factors. In our terminology, to get at PHIL we have to exclude KRAT(1) and KRAT(2) factors. Hence the form of our assessment must be such as to allow S to reflect, at leisure, on what he thinks ought to be done—on what criterion he thinks appropriate (whether that of other people's interests or some other). It is, indeed, necessary to ensure that S (particularly if S is a young child with low verbal ability) *understands* the story or other test-form; in that sense, the situation must be 'made real' to him. But it is equally necessary to ensure that it is not too life-like. If, for instance, we used some game- or simulation-situation instead of a pencil-and-paper story, S would be more likely to be carried away by 'in-the-field' [KRAT(1) and (2)] factors, although we could of course use a simulation-situation, or a film, or puppets, or some other non-verbal presentation provided we allowed S time to reflect on it. But we

1. ERE, Ch. 10.

have throughout to remember that our aim is to get at S's *general* moral views.

In order to do this we shall of course have to present S with other options, with other criteria besides the 'other people's interests' criterion. This means that we shall present him with conflict-situations, in which he may be tempted to opt for other criteria. We need for this an adequate typology of what other criteria are likely to operate. This will be of particular importance in determining whether S's views are overriding, and we can only determine this by making available not only the practical syllogism in which we are interested ('One ought to act in others' interests: this is in others' interests: there do this'), but also other practical syllogisms (e.g. 'One ought to seek one's own advantage', 'One ought not to lose face', 'One ought not to disobey authority', 'One ought to act the way one's friends do', etc. as major premisses).

We have also to remember that the test-form will not be primarily concerned with what specific action S thinks right, but with S's *reasons*: that is, with whether S chooses the action in virtue of the criterion of others' interests. It is very easy to forget this point in an endeavour to keep test-stories simple and easily-scorable. We may ask numerous questions of the form, 'What should Johnny do?' or 'What ought you to do?', forgetting that the answers to these are *only* relevant if we can be certain that they show the operation of a certain reason or criterion; and this need not be so. Even in conflict-situations, S may have all kinds of reasons for choosing what is (accidentally) the 'right answer'—in terms of others' interests— reasons quite disconnected logically from that criterion. We have to make sure that the criterion is actually being used.

Now it is fairly obvious that few if any Ses will always get the 'right answer' for the right reasons. An S will to some extent, or in some spheres, or some situations, claim the criterion of others' interests, but in other situations deploy some other criterion. How are we to cater for this, either in devising or scoring the assessments? To this there is no simple answer. What we have to do is to make sensible guesses about the possible categories in which Ses may vary in their application of the criterion. For example, it is a fairly safe bet that some Ses will apply it in situations concerned with members of their own family or gang, but not outside; whites, but not to blacks, and so on. We have here a category or dimension which we shall call *range;* and I shall now go on, not without some hesitation, to sketch out such factors. I must stress, however, that although all these categories (and no doubt others) need to be tried out in assessment, it is at present quite unclear which of them will turn out to be of the most practical significance.

A. *Range*. This concerns the numbers and classes of people for whom S applies the criterion. Important categories here may be *similarity* to S (in age, sex, social class, tastes, etc.); *social distance* (whether the other is a family- or gang- or class-member); *social behaviour* of the other (whether 'nice' or 'nasty'); *appearance* or *manner* of the other (physical attraction, accent, etc.); *social status* of the other; *age* or *sex* of the other.

B. *Situation-similarity*. This turns on whether S has himself been in situations like that given in the story, where S has needed others to attend to his interests (e.g. S has often needed financial help himself, and is perhaps more likely to say that a story-person should have it).

C. *Situation-experience*: whether S has experienced situations similar to the story-situation (irrespective of whether S has himself been in a position of need, as in B. above).

D. *Harming and helping*. An S may perform well at not-harming, but badly at helping, or vice versa.

E. *Subject-matter*. The empirical *type* of harm or help may be important. Among these types we may list:
 (i) 'bodily' (violence, food, sex)
 (ii) 'property' (stealing, lending money)
(iii) 'nuisance/kindness' (excessive noise, baby-sitting without payment)
(iv) 'words' (slander, cheering someone up)
 (v) 'contract' (lying, keeping promises, punctuality, debts)

F. *Scope/distribution*. S may use the criterion well in distributing 'goods' to others, but badly when allowing others power or scope (in voting, decision-making), or vice versa.

G. *Visible immediacy*. S may use the criterion well when the results are visibly immediate, badly when the results—though immediate in point of time—cannot be seen: e.g. not stealing from friends, but stealing from the railways or the taxpayer.

H. *Temporal immediacy*. As above, but in respect of time: e.g. S may be concerned about the good of others now or for the immediate future, but not about the eventual results of pollution, overpopulation, etc.

It should be clear that these categories are by no means exhaustive. But they are important, not only for PHIL but for other components also; and we shall find ourselves referring to them as we proceed. I have not extended them, chiefly because the most sensible procedure is to begin by trying out tests and assessments that take these at least into account, and then (with the help of interviews and information derived from conversation and behavioural observation) get clearer about which categories are most significant. Only by spreading the net wide enough shall we ever be in a position to give S a *general* rating for this aspect of PHIL; and even this may prove unwise. For S's claim to the criterion may be *so* specific to particular situations (or other types of category) that we may be able to do no more than rate S within the various categories.

I have not added the point made earlier about conflict-situations and the possibility of other 'overriding syllogisms' to the list above, because this point is of a different order of importance. The list contains a selection of *other* factors that may affect S's use of the criterion: and some of these other factors will themselves be such as to generate other 'overriding syllogisms' for S. But it should now go without saying that we must, above all, take care to include in our stories (or whatever presentations we use) the various 'pulls' of guilt, honour, self-advantage, and so forth.

It should also be unnecessary to say that, since we are concerned here with one aspect of PHIL only, we must control for other components (as well as, of course, for other variables such as IQ, reading ability, etc.). Thus we are here interested in what S *thinks* to be in the other's interests; whether S is correct or not may turn on his factual knowledge (GIG) or knowledge of others' emotions (EMP). We may best control for these by so simplifying the story that all Ses may be presumed to have adequate EMP and GIG. We cannot wholly exclude S's 'bring-to-bear' component [KRAT (1)], since we are after all getting S to bring his knowledge and principles to bear in one, albeit very restricted, situation: namely, the test-situation. But by giving S plenty of time, and keeping the presentation simple enough, nearly all Ses should have sufficient KRAT(1) for us to feel secure. We are, in effect, doing the 'bringing-to-bear' for S, precisely by presenting him with the test (plus whatever incentives are required to ensure that S does it properly).

## 3. Rule-supporting feelings

We turn now to a very different aspect of PHIL. Let us assume that S has the required concept of a person, and claims this concept as a moral principle of rule of behaviour. It may still be the case that S has little or no *feeling* attached to this rule, and little or no tendency to *act* in accordance with it. We are here concerned with the former (feeling), but the general point requires a brief discussion.

It is perfectly true that, if an S said that he believed he ought to decide and act by the criterion of others' interests, but rarely or never did so, and rarely or never showed remorse, guilt, or sorrow at not having done so, or pleasure or self-approval when he did so— then, in this (rare) case, we should be tempted to say that S could not have really meant what he first said. 'Could not', not because there is a tight logical entailment between believing that one ought to do something on the one hand, and doing it and having certain feelings on the other—there need be no such entailment unless we force one: but because characteristically (rather than necessarily) humans tend to do, and to have certain feelings about, what they think they ought to do. Hence we should be justly suspicious, to say the least, of the S quoted above. But it is still possible (indeed common) *in certain cases* for an S to assent sincerely to our criterion, and yet neither to act on it nor to have certain feelings about it.[1]

For these reasons it is necessary to deal with the feelings and action under separate headings. This is all the more required of us, because in section 2 above we were concerned solely with what we called S's 'moral theory', his intellectual opinion (so to speak) about what criterion he thought he ought to use—as an overriding and prescriptive criterion, certainly, but not necessarily as the one he actually *did* use. We need, then, to find out how far the criterion actually *is* supported by some kind of commitment on S's part. We shall here deal with the extent of what I call S's 'rule-supporting feelings': S's 'rule-derived' decisions and actions will come under KRAT(1) and (2).

Note further that we are concerned with S's feelings only insofar as they are subordinated to the rule about others' interests. The feelings must be for the other *as for* a being with rights, interests, needs, etc. It is *about the other's interests* that he must feel (and act), not about the other under some other description or in some other light. For instance, I may hold as a principle that others' interests should be satisfied: I may satisfy the interests of an attractive blonde, and I may also have strong feelings about her. But my feelings are not about her *as* a source of needs or interests; and I am not here acting *on* my principle, but only moved to act in what happens to be in accordance with it. My sexual feelings for the blonde are not 'rule-supporting' feelings. Again, there may be something about the sight of a cripple which moves me in some way (I feel embarrassed or guilty) such that I give him money; but I am not necessarily

1. ERE, Ch. 10.

giving him money because his interests require that I should.

Nevertheless we must distinguish here between two types of feelings, which I shall call 'duty-orientated' (DO) and 'person-orientated' (PO). This distinction is not between the S who uses the rule about others' interests as a criterion for action and the S who does not: both must govern their actions by the rule. The latter S could not be said to have PHIL or to show genuine benevolence or love, however sentimental or affectionate or strongly-moved he might be towards another person, precisely because he does not control his behaviour by the rule. Nor, again, is the distinction between the S who will do his (contractual) duty but no more, and the S who will go further: for our concept of others' interests extends indefinitely, beyond any contractual duty (though not excluding it). The 'duty-orientated' S may look after the interests of the starving Chinese as well as of his family; the 'person-orientated' S may only look after his family. The distinction is rather in the *kind* of feelings that accompany S's obedience to the rule.

This difference of kind does not lie in the *strength* of the feeling. An S who is DO may feel very strongly (in a Kantian sort of way) about the importance of doing his duty, of attending to the rule about others' interests, but what he will lack is the PO feelings which should, in *some* cases at least, accompany his attention to others. For those latter feelings we use words like 'sympathy', 'love', 'affection', 'identification with others'. Perhaps a good way of putting it is to say that S should *take pleasure* in the other, that S should be happy, not that he has done his duty, but that the other is happy.

The importance of this aspect of PHIL has been mentioned elsewhere.[1] Briefly, there are many contexts in human life—particularly in such close relationships as marriage and child-rearing—where others' interests are served not so much by action as by feeling of a PO type. Wives and children, for instance, may care less about getting presents than about their husbands' or fathers' affection. This is not to say that there may not be other contexts (e.g. having to conduct a surgical operation, or organize relief supplies to disaster areas) where affection either does not count, or positively inhibits the effective performance of the required task.

We have, then, to assess these DO and PO feelings. It is worth nothing that we cannot assess them simply by observing what S does. S may have the relevant feelings, yet those feelings may not be overriding: they may not issue in action. For instance, S1 may be

1. IME, pp. 59–67.

very sorry for the Jews in Nazi Germany, yet be even more frightened of what might happen to him if he actually helped them; S2 may be less sorry for the Jews, but because he has no fear at all may actually help the Jews. Here S1's PHIL-feelings are stronger than S2's, but do not issue in action. We have, then, to assess the DO and PO feelings independently of behaviour—though this is not, of course, to say that we cannot use behavioural observations to induce such feelings, provided we are sure that our inductions are correct.

One important difference between assessment in this area, as opposed to that in section 2 above, is that we cannot do other than try to assess the feelings of S 'in the field'; that is, we are trying to get at what S feels in real-life situations. Our presentations, therefore, will not be designed so much to give S leisure to reflect, since reflection is not relevant: what we want to know is how much rule-supporting feeling actually attaches itself to the criterion of others' interests. Apart from field observation, therefore, we shall be inclined to use simulation- or participation-situations, practical experiments, visual media and other methods that try to reproduce real-life situations as far as possible.

What then are these 'rule-supporting' feelings? Chief among them will be *remorse* or *guilt* when S does not follow a rule, *self-approbation* or *pleasure* when S does follow it, *disapproval* when S sees someone else not following the rule, and *sorrow* or *regret* or *pity* in respect of the person whose needs are unsatisfied, *approval* and *pleasure* at rule-keeping and the other's satisfaction. These and other relevant feelings have their characteristic beliefs, symptoms and actions[1] (weeping, making restitution, smiles, frowns, etc.) and can be assessed, although with difficulty. Such difficulty should make us incline towards many different kinds of assessment (self-reporting, interviews, behavioural observation, reporting from peers and others who know S well, and so on), and those contexts of assessment which seem best able to give us the information we need.

## Summary

Above we have distinguished three sub-components of PHIL, the third of which is divided into two. These were:

(1) having the concept of a 'person'. I shall call this PHIL(HC).
(2) claiming the concept as a moral principle. PHIL(CC).
(3) having rule-supporting feelings, 'duty-orientated' or 'person-orientated'. PHIL(RSF-DO) and PHIL(RSF-PO).

1. Kenny (1963): ERE, Ch. 7.

## EMP

Under the heading EMP we are concerned with the area often described in such terms as 'emotional awareness', 'sensitivity', 'insight', 'empathy', etc.

## 1. Having the concepts of emotion

To have the concept of an emotion is a necessary precondition for being able, in practice, to identify the emotion. S must know what jealousy *is* if S is to be able to know that so-and-so is jealous. This at once raises questions about what emotions are, and what the particular emotions are. I and other writers have dealt with these elsewhere;[1] here I shall give merely what is likely to be of use to empirical researchers and test-constructors.

First, there are important distinctions between emotions and other similar mental phenomena which we may prefer to call 'moods', 'states of mind', 'motives', 'wants', or, more generally, 'feelings'. Emotions, necessarily or characteristically, have *targets* (not just causes), and have a 'cognitive core' consisting of a *belief*; 'moods' (happiness, depression) do not. Under EMP in general we shall include not only emotions in the strict sense, but 'wants', 'moods', etc. as well; but the distinction will obviously be important for testing purposes.

Secondly, the concept of an emotion is usually made up of the following elements:

(a) a belief (that X is dangerous)
(b) involuntary or semi-voluntary symptoms (trembling, going pale), including certain postures, gestures, facial expressions, etc.
(c) intentional action (running away, trying to avoid attention).

Emotions may be recognized, in ourselves and others, by these three ways. They may also, under normal conditions, be recognized by the *surrounding circumstances*. Thus, to fit the example of fear above, we can induce that X feels fear if we know that a bull is chasing X, or an avalanche is coming towards X, and that X is aware of this.

Thirdly, to have the concept of a particular emotion (as was pointed out under PHIL earlier) involves being able to classify the phenomena in (a), (b) and (c) above under a single criterion. Usually the grasp of an emotion-concept will be represented by an

1. ERE, Ch. 7 (with refs., especially to Kenny and Peters).

ordinary word—'anger', 'fear', 'remorse', etc. But this is not a necessary condition. If we ask S what X is feeling, and S says 'Well, it's what people feel when someone else has something nice which they feel is somehow rightfully theirs: such people tend to say such-and-such and act in such-and-such ways', etc., then it does not matter that S does not know the *word* 'jealousy': he has the concept. Also it is not required, just for having the concept, that S is any good at identifying emotions in practice. In order to test for this [as for PHIL(HC)] we should have to 'hold the information steady', so to speak: that is, ensure that Ses all had the same information, in order to find out whether they could classify it under appropriate concepts.

Fourthly, there are, of course, a number of very different emotions and hence different concepts. S may have the concepts of fear, anger and hate, but not of remorse or pride. We shall have to assess for all emotion-concepts, or at least for a representative sample (if we know what a representative sample would look like). This is not as bad as it sounds, for the number of basic emotions and moods is finite and in fact fairly small. What we require for this is a reliable taxonomy of the emotions, a task that badly needs undertaking. But the empirical researcher will not go far wrong if he starts, at least, by devising assessments for the most common and obvious emotions.

Finally, it may seem odd to suggest that there can be Ses who do not have the concepts of such emotions as fear, anger, etc.: only mythical heroes, or those very ignorant of English, ask 'What is fear?' No doubt this is generally true. But it is not at all clear, at least in some cases, whether a 'psychopathic' S (whatever this means) merely does not *feel*, say, remorse, or whether he also lacks the *concept*. Further, there may be many Ses who lack the concepts for the more complex emotions (jealousy and envy, remorse and regret, pride and vanity), emotions about which, indeed, we may require to get a good deal clearer than we are. Both for research and, ultimately, for teaching purposes, this aspect of EMP is far from unimportant.

## 2. Being able to identify one's own emotions (conscious and unconscious) and other people's (conscious and unconscious)

We are dealing here with what we shall later demarcate as four separate sub-components of EMP: but the relevant logical points are too closely connected to separate. The reader will find them discussed fully elsewhere.[1]

1. ERE, Chs. 8–10.

First, we are talking about *abilities*. Can S, in practice, correctly say, e.g. 'I am feeling insecure', 'He is jealous', 'She is frightened', etc.? S may have this ability, but not bring it to bear [for lack of KRAT(1)]. To test this ability we should have to hold the 'motivation'—that is, simply how much incentive S has to use the ability—constant. This is a problem usually either not faced or not solved in much psychological research (for instance, in intelligence tests).

Secondly, we are not concerned with *how* S knows what he or others feel. There is a temptation to think that S has a different *kind* of knowledge in his own case—a 'direct', 'self-authenticating', 'intuitive' or 'certain' knowledge. This is not so.[1] S is differently placed for acquiring knowledge of his own feelings, as against other people's: but this placing has both advantages and disadvantages. Sometimes S will know better than other people what he feels, or what they feel; sometimes not. We are concerned only with *whether* he knows.

Thirdly, S's knowledge is bound to consist in noting, and probably in correlating, the various aspects of emotions that we noticed in 1 above: that is, the belief, symptoms, actions, and surrounding circumstances that go to make up the emotion. Our assessment will be based largely on this. S will be able or unable to induce from (say) facial expressions or postures to beliefs, or from beliefs to actions, or from actions to symptoms. Not much is known about the ways in which this ability operates, but obviously assessors must make use of any relevant research.

Fourthly, it is likely that Ses will perform variably, depending on the particular emotion, the context in which they are called on to identify it, the people of whom they predicate the emotion, and so forth, as well as being more or less good at making inductions from the various signs of emotion mentioned above. We shall need, then, a list not unlike that given for PHIL(CC), which takes account of the various areas, contexts, classes of people and so forth. Thus S1 may be no good at identifying emotions in women; S2 may be baffled by the over-40s; S3 inept when dealing with societies of men whose facial expressions are in some respects unlike those common in our own culture; and so on. I shall not attempt such a list here, but will sketch out some possibly important categories when we turn to practical assessment.

Fifthly, it needs to be made plain that we are not only concerned with this ability in face-to-face situations. The morally educated S

---

1. Some philosophers seem disposed to deny this. I have tried to say a little about it in Appendix II.

must know what a person would be likely to feel, or to have felt, in the (real or imaginary) future or past. He must be able to *imagine*, as well as (in some sense) *see*, the emotions of himself and of others. This plainly involves different (and in some ways easier) methods of assessment.

Sixthly (and this is connected with our second point above), it is not of course required that S actually *feel* the emotions which he knows to exist in the other person. It may be, indeed, that those Ses who can 'put themselves in other people's shoes' are in fact better at EMP (and perhaps at PHIL also) if they can do this in a strong sense: that is, to *have* something like the other's feelings ('empathy'?) rather than just being able to state correctly what the other feels. This may be highly relevant to *methods* of developing EMP and PHIL: but it is not what we are testing for here.

Finally, the distinction between conscious and unconscious emotions requires a brief note. Sidestepping many problems discussed elsewhere,[1] I shall here mean by 'conscious' emotions those which the person who has the emotion would *not* require any lengthy process of psychotherapy to recognize, and those which he is not prevented from knowing by any deep-laid defences or resistances. For instance, suppose I am angry. I may not be conscious of my anger in the sense of being able to say at once 'Yes, I'm angry', but I could without too much difficulty see that I was trembling, shouting, attacking and (perhaps) that I believed someone was thwarting me. If I have difficulty, I lack EMP in respect of my conscious emotions: I am not good, in practice, at noting and correlating the symptoms, actions, etc. of anger in myself (or perhaps in others). The 'raw material' is available to me, but I do not make use of it. On the other hand, the 'raw material' of unconscious emotions (in myself and others) is more subtle and hidden: neither I nor they could reasonably be expected to have it available and to hand immediately. Yet I may induce unconscious emotions, if I have a lot of EMP in this particular area. Naturally Ses may vary a great deal depending on whether it is their own or others' conscious or unconscious emotions: hence we divide this into four sub-components.

The distinction between conscious and unconscious is not an absolute one: we might rather talk in terms of degrees of availability. Nevertheless, a rough distinction between the two may be made, similar to that which we shall make when dealing with KRAT(1) and KRAT(2). It is sense, though untidy, to talk of what is 'nor-

1. ERE, Ch. 9,

mally' available consciousness, just as it is sense to talk of 'bring to bear' [KRAT(1)] one's conscious principles and faculties, though there may be unconscious 'parts of oneself' which one has not 'brought to bear'. It would be unobjectionable, perhaps, if we collapsed these four sub-components into two, abolishing the conscious-unconscious distinction, and giving a range of assessments that ran from the 'immediately available' to the 'deeply hidden'. But I should be inclined to keep the fourfold division firmly in mind.

A more serious difficulty may be that assessors may not know, in the case of unconscious emotions, what the 'right answers' are. The very existence of unconscious emotions, and the sense of that phrase, are both disputed: and what unconscious emotions are felt by whom, and on what occasions, is disputed much more. Nevertheless, there seem to be some clear cases. There is, for instance, the adolescent who (unconsciously) feels insecure, impotent, frightened, and who behaves like a 'tough guy', keeps measuring his strength against authority, and so forth, perhaps consciously feeling nothing but contempt and hatred for the adult world of which he is secretly envious and scared. There is the Casanova who consciously despises women, but unconsciously is in desperate need of them. There is the 'nice chap' who consciously likes other people, but unconsciously fears them and tries to placate them. Of course, assessors would have to agree, and to agree for good reasons, on the 'right answers'. But this whole area is of such importance to moral education that the attempt seems well worth making.[1]

## Summary

We have distinguished five sub-components of EMP. These were:

(1) Having the concepts of emotions, 'moods', etc. This I call EMP(HC).
(2) Being able to identify conscious emotions in oneself—EMP(1)(Cs)

Being able to identify unconscious emotions in oneself—EMP(1)(Ucs)

Being able to identify conscious emotions in others—EMP(2)(Cs)

Being able to identify unconscious emotions in others—EMP(2)(Ucs)

## GIG

This is perhaps the easiest component to deal with, and we can be fairly brief.

1. ERE, Ch. 9.

## 1. Knowing relevant 'hard' facts and sources of facts

Under this heading we exclude EMP, which deserved a separate treatment. By 'hard' facts I intend to exclude awareness of emotions and moods (EMP) but to include sensations (an S who does not know that a hard slap on the back may hurt a girl lacks this quality). Most of the 'relevant facts', however, will not be directly concerned with sensations of people, but with the following basic categories:

(i) *Facts relating to health, safety, etc.* This is a large category, and includes such things as what drugs are addictive, elementary biology, first aid, contraceptive devices, the danger of certain machines (cars, electrical devices), what to do in case of fire, and so on.

(ii) *Laws, social norms, conventions, etc.* This includes what may be called 'social facts': not only the law of the land, but also the conventions and etiquette of particular social groups with which S may be in contact, the particular powers and scope of various authorities, the workings of particular institutions, social rules and so on.

(iii) *Facts about individuals or groups in need.* S needs to know, not just what is (as a matter of 'hard' fact) required in general to satisfy others' interests, but also about the existence of various others who are in need. It is relevant that there are old people, starving people, etc. in other countries, or in some other way removed from S's immediate environment.

It is not altogether easy to draw a sharp distinction between this quality and EMP. Under EMP we include awareness of wants as well as emotions, and it might be argued that this overlaps in certain cases—perhaps particularly in (ii) above. Nevertheless, knowledge of laws, conventions and expectations can be roughly distinguished from awareness of wants. In practice we can reasonably confine ourselves here to the 'hard' facts relating to *need* or *requirements*. Whether a person *wants* a certain medicine if he is ill, or wants the kind of politeness that is conventional in his group, is here irrelevant: S will still find it useful to know what medicine the person *needs* or what is socially appropriate.

In reference to (iii), we need also to remember that EMP is relevant only when S knows that a person exists, and knows something about him (so that he has, as it were, some chance of knowing what the person feels). It is the 'hard' knowledge of the person's (or group's) existence and circumstances with which we are concerned under (iii).

Turning to 'sources' of facts, I intend here to make some allowance, so to speak, for those who happen to be ill-informed in particular areas. S may not know much about medicine, but it will make a big difference whether he approaches the doctor or the witch-doctor when he or another is ill. He may not know much about science, but it is important whether he asks the physicist or the priest. Ses who are children or teenagers may rely on their friends as sources of knowledge, rather than their parents or teachers. In general, what we are after here is some awareness on S's part that X or Y is the *kind* of thing that comes under some general heading ('economics', 'medicine', 'science'): that there is some expertise here. Straightforward sources of knowledge, such as the encyclopaedia, are also not to be despised. The three general groups given above will operate for this kind of knowledge also: it is the same facts that we want him either himself to know, or to know how to find out.

To some extent, it will be true that 'relevant' knowledge is different for different Ses. It does not count much against my moral education if I do not know the conventions current among pygmy tribes, or much against a pygmy's if he does not know the social expectations of an Oxford sherry party. If S's own group is at semi-starvation level, S may be pardoned for not taking a great interest in the needs of what count as poor people in the UK. In this respect (and perhaps in this only) our tests are trying to measure something which is not demanded *in the same form* of all cultures. But it is still *equally* demanded. In other words, 'relevant facts' are equally important for me and for pygmies, but the content of this title will be different: whereas, for other components, not only the general quality but the specific content will be the same (emotions, having interests, 'relevant alertness', etc. are common to all societies). In any case, since there are many fundamental similarities between human beings in respect of these 'hard' facts, particular in the area of health and safety, much of the test-content will be common. (When we meet Martians it may be another matter.)

## 2. 'Knowing how': non-propositional skills in dealing with people

In relationships with people there is an important 'skill' element, which may be present or absent independently of the propositional knowledge of EMP, or of the 'hard-fact' knowledge mentioned just above. We are talking here of a skill which cannot be wholly learned by learning the truth or reasons of various propositions, but which might be picked up in practice or by imitation (like learning to swim). I am thinking here of such contexts as apologising, cheering someone up, displaying sympathy, giving or receiving orders, and so forth. Of course propositional knowledge may improve S's abilities in such contexts, but we are here concerned to assess only the 'skill' element, so that such knowledge must be held constant. We have also, of course, to hold constant the motivational factors [KRAT(1)]: for we are interested in S's ability only—whether he can, not whether he wants to.

These skills may be divided into (a) verbal communication skills, and (b) non-verbal communication skills. (a) is about whether S says the right thing (when apologising, ordering, etc.); (b) about whether he says it in the right tone of voice, with the right stance, gestures, etc. Both (a) and (b) are concerned with what S *does*, but not with what S does deliberately. For example, S1 may (unconsciously) always stand the right distance away from the person he talks to, smile at the right times, etc., and this will count as well as S2's deliberate taking-up of position and smiling. If S3, however, is liked or disliked for what he *is* (badly-dressed, ugly, dwarfish), this does not count. The distinction is a fine one, but may be drawn well enough in practice. We have to draw it in order to demarcate this quality at all: for it is something in respect of which people can be trained or educated, and we must exclude cases where Ses may be more or less acceptable to others for quite different reasons. (Being an attractive blonde is not a social skill.)

## Summary

We have distinguished:
Knowledge of relevant 'hard' facts. We call this GIG(1)(KF).
Knowledge of sources of facts: GIG(1)(KS).
'Knowing-how', or 'social skills' of verbal communication: GIG(2)(VC).
Ditto for non-verbal communication: GIG(2)(NVC).

## KRAT(1)

We have here perhaps the most complicated of the components. In dealing with PHIL, we first wanted to know whether S had the concept of a person in the required sense [PHIL(HC)], and then whether S thought he ought to apply this concept in the sense of acting in accordance with others' interests [PHIL(CC)]. Both

these components could be described as 'cognitive', in that we are
not concerned with any feelings or tendencies to act or behaviour
on the part of S, except in the possible but unusual case of an S
who said he thought he ought to act in others' interests, but never
(or hardly ever) did so—in this case we should have doubts about
S's sincerity. There is, then, no very tight conceptual connection
between PHIL(HC) and (CC) and S's actual feelings or behaviour
in 'real life'.

With PHIL(RSF), however, there is a stronger connection. An S
who has some feelings, whether of a 'duty-orientated' or 'person-
orientated' kind (DO or PO), that support the rule of acting in
others' interests *eo ipso* has some motive or incentive for doing so.
And the stronger the feelings—the more PHIL(RSF)—the more
we should normally expect that he did so. But there is still not a
necessary conceptual connection here. First, S may have the
feelings, but not have them as rule-supporting feelings *in practice*.
That is, it may be that when S considers, in the abstract, what he
thinks he ought in general to do, he has feelings which support the
PHIL(CC) rule, but that when he is called upon to decide and
act in real life, he either does not have these feelings or does not
have them *as* rule-supporting feelings. Secondly, S may have the
feelings as RSF, but the feelings are not powerful enough for them
to be overriding, in the sense of issuing in *action*. Yet they may still
be powerful. S1 has a strong incentive to help a person, but he has a
stronger feeling of embarrassment and so fails to do so. S2 has a
weaker incentive but no embarrassment, and so helps the person.

For these (and other) reasons we need a separate component,
which we call KRAT(1). This is generally concerned with 'bringing
to bear' the previous components when S is actually faced with the
need for decision and action, with whether S's attitudes and abilities
and attainments, listed under PHIL, EMP, and GIG are 'alive'
in real-life situations. For it is clearly possible that they should be
inert. This is easy to see in the case of EMP and GIG: S may have
emotional awareness, the ability to identify others' feelings, but not
actually use it (through laziness, nervousness or many other reasons);
and S may know all the relevant facts, and have all the 'social
skills', but not make use of the knowledge and skills when it comes
to the point. As we have seen, this applies to PHIL also. We all
know many Ses who quite genuinely hold, as a sincere moral
theory, that they ought to act in others' interests, and who (to a
greater or lesser degree) have genuine feelings which relate to
and to some degree activate this rule, but who, nonetheless, sometimes or even often fail to follow the rule in practice.

Failure to follow the rule in practice may be of two kinds. Either S fails even to reach the stage of making a proper *decision*, and this is what we are concerned with under KRAT(1); or else he makes a decision, but fails to carry it out even though it was within his power, and this we shall leave to KRAT(2). The 'decision' we are talking about here, however, needs to be specified more fully. It is not just a question of S thinking that X ought to be done 'in principle', as it were: it is a question of S's committing himself to action in making the decision. We shall expand on this later: here I want to show the width and nature of the gap that KRAT(1) has to fill, between S's just 'having' PHIL, EMP and GIG, and S's making what I have so far called only a 'proper' decision.

The first way in which S can fail to bridge the gap is simply by not being *alert* or not *noticing* that a decision is required. S may be in a daydream, or so intent on his own ends that he does not even realize that a moral situation confronts him. By a 'moral situation' here I mean a situation in which others' interests are at stake, and S can act in their favour. This shows that what we require here is not just that S should be, as it were, generally 'alert', but that he should be *relevantly* alert: that is, alert to certain classes of situation. Moreover, he would not count as being 'relevantly alert' if he did not see the situation *under the right description*. If some poor chap is being pelted with stones, S may notice this and say 'How amusing!', and whilst there might perhaps be a correct description under which it *was* amusing, nevertheless we want S to see it as a case of another person in need of help, suffering, etc. We shall describe this part of KRAT(1) as 'relevant alertness', and call it KRAT(1) (RA).

The second type of failure, closely connected but distinguishable, is if S fails to *think thoroughly* about the situation to which he has alerted himself. A bell rings in S's mind, so to speak, whenever it might seem as if others' interests were at stake: but then S might not bother to think much further about the situation. He might fail to make full and proper use of his PHIL, EMP and GIG— particular, in this sub-component, of his EMP and GIG. S should ask himself questions like 'What does this person really feel? Is it really a desire to help him that I myself feel, or some other desire? What facts do I know, or could I find out, that would make my help effective?', and so on. (I do not imply, of course, that S has always to do all this *consciously*.) Here it is important to note that S will summon up *any* ability, skill, attainment, etc. that he possesses— e.g., not just what he does know, but what he could find out. This part of KRAT(1) we shall call 'thinking thoroughly'—KRAT(1) (TT).

Thirdly, when S reaches the stage of making a decision, he may fail in three ways. (a) His decision may not be the result of his PHIL being *overriding*. Despite his KRAT(1)(RA) and (TT), there may still be some other overriding syllogism derived from his own self-interest, or his inner feelings of guilt, or whatever, which prevents him from deciding in accordance with, and because of, the PHIL principle about others' interests. (b) His decision may not be thoroughly *prescriptive*: that is, S may think in a general sort of way that X ought to be done, but not that *he himself* ought to do it. S is required, as it were, to command or prescribe the required action to himself: to commit himself to acting. (c) His decision may be such that he thinks that *he* ought to do X, but not that X is the thing that *anyone* in a similar position ought to do. S's rule must not be a rule for himself alone, but must be universalizable. (These last two requirements might perhaps be put by saying that S must mean 'ought' in a full sense.) From the requirement that S's decision should be overriding, prescriptive and universalizable we shall describe this aspect of KRAT(1) as KRAT(1)(OPU).

The assessment of KRAT(1), in its RA, TT and OPU aspects, is beset by similar complications to those of PHIL(CC). That is, there is likely to be a great variety of performance depending on various categories (the type of situation, the people involved, etc.); but we have also an added difficulty. S's decision to act can, obviously, be to some extent verified by seeing how S actually does act. However, we need to know that S acts *as a result of* this kind of decision; we need to know what 'goes on in S's head'. So mere observation of behaviour, even coupled with assessments of PHIL (CC) and (RSF), will not be enough: we shall need interviews, cross-questioning of S, and so forth. Such methods will be even more necessary if we are to distinguish whether S lacks the RA, TT or OPU elements of KRAT(1), and, in the latter case, we should need to know whether it was the O, P or U element that was lacking.[1]

A few lines above we mentioned the problems caused by variety of context or situation. For KRAT(1) there will be some important additions to be made to the list given for PHIL(CC).[2] This is (obviously) because, in the latter case, there are no serious problems about the *context in which* S 'claims the concept', though of course there are problems about the *internal* situation (e.g. the elements in the story) about which S is asked to judge. Thus a test for PHIL(CC) might be in the form of a story in which S's 'peer group' or friends

1. ERE, Ch. 10.
2. pp. 45–6.

pull one way, and others' interests another way. But the peer group is not present in person when S chooses one or the other criterion. With KRAT(1), however, this is not so. S's peers are present, perhaps, looking at him, jeering, shouting 'Come on!', leaving him isolated, and so on, and this is a very different matter.

What we are looking for here are categories and contexts which (we guess) so alter the surrounding circumstances of S's decision that we should expect very different 'scores' for KRAT(1) in different categories. Perhaps, in particular, we are looking for *special* or *atypical* circumstances. We may reasonably entertain the concept of S 'normally' bringing to bear, or not bringing to bear, his PHIL, EMP and GIG so as to reach a decision, and go on to determine the 'special circumstances' which encourage S to behave abnormally. S's 'normal score', of course, will depend on general features of S's personality, his 'rule-supporting feelings', general attitude to other people, and so on: these are not 'special circumstances' in any sense. If S is characteristically nervous of other people, over-anxious, apathetic, hostile, etc. then these will affect (rightly) his 'normal' score.

The following categories, which may be taken just as general categories analogous to those suggested for PHIL(CC) or as 'special circumstance' categories, seem to be possibly relevant for assessment:

(a) *Influence of 'potent' others.* I use this jargon-term to refer to 'others' who might, for normal Ses, exercise particular influence on his decision-making 'in the field': e.g. S's peer group, his parents or other authority-figures, his girl-friend, his dependants. These will affect S's KRAT(1) in ways more familiar to the social psychologist than to myself.

(b) *Influence of locale.* It is likely to make a big difference whether S's decision is taken in his own country or abroad; at home or at school; at work or at play; conceivably, in a crowded city or in the open country; and so on.

(c) *Influence of immediately prior experience.* If S has, for instance, just scored a notable success at school or, conversely, been severely rebuked in front of his class-mates, won a sweepstake or had a row with his wife, seen an amusing film or been bored to tears by X's conversation—these and suchlike will affect the issue.

(d) *Influence of temporary 'moods'.* It will matter whether S feels depressed at that particular time, elated, 'unreal', and so on. There are temporary moods of this kind which are *not* caused by immediately prior experiences [as in (c)].

I am only too aware that the above four categories are very unsophisticated. There will be borderline cases and cross-categorizations (e.g. if S is *with* his peer group *in* a football stadium *when* his favoured team has just lost, *and* S is 'in a bad mood' that day anyway. This seems to bring in all four categories).

## KRAT(2)

If S has KRAT(1), as well as the other components, he reaches the DIK-stage: that is, the stage of making a 'proper' decision to act in others' interests. But he may still not do so. For reasons given elsewhere,[1] it is both logically and empirically possible for S to make a sincere and genuine decision and not to carry it out even though he could do so. If we put enough weight (against normal usage) on such concepts as sincerity, genuineness, wholeheartedness, 'bringing to bear', 'prescriptive', etc., then we can deny that this is true, and say that S will necessarily act unless he is prevented. But I have argued that to do this is to direct our attention away from a very important class of cases which is of particular interest to the researcher.

This is the class of cases in which S has made a 'proper' (sincere, etc.) decision, but does not carry it out, *not* because he is in any simple sense prevented (as if his hands were tied behind his back), but because there is some unconscious counter-motivation or counter-syllogism. On what seems to me to be the correct view of the unconscious, we shall say that there is a part of S—so unknown to himself that we cannot properly speak of S's decision as 'insincere' —that is *following different rules*; or we can say, if we like, that S himself (unconsciously) follows different rules, as a result of unconscious beliefs and emotions. This is, obviously, a very different view of the unconscious than that held by some, particularly by those who regard it as a clumsy way of talking about conditioned reflexes, 'imprinting', etc. On our view, it is often the case not that S cannot, but that in an important sense S does not *want* to, perform the required action.

Since the unconscious is, on this view, in principle educable, and since there is a sense (which I shall not expand here) in which S is responsible and perhaps 'to blame' for the rules he unconsciously follows, and since, further, this class of cases seems to me very large, it would be a mistake to exclude it from consideration. We are, then, dealing with cases in which S has got as far as KRAT(1), to the

---

1. ERE, Ch. 10.

DIK-stage: but then S simply does not (does not want to, rather than cannot) do what he ought, or what he has sincerely decided. But it will be immediately apparent that there is very little the philosopher can say about this class of cases. We could, no doubt, attempt some kind of taxonomy of the various unconscious counter-syllogisms that may be operating, but this seems rather a task for the clinical psychologist or psychoanalyst.

For our purposes of assessment, all we can do (and it is enough) is to identify that it is in *this* area that S fails. We shall describe the area as KRAT(2), because of its similarity with KRAT(1). We can assess it, at least by any direct form of assessment, only by determining that S has made a 'proper' decision, by assuring ourselves that there is no straightforward prevention of S's acting, and then by seeing whether S does or does not act. If S does not, he lacks KRAT(2). We shall of course take care to confine ourselves to standard cases, where a 'normal' or reasonably well-integrated person (I shall not enlarge on these phrases here) would be expected to carry out his decision.

## Status of the components

I have pointed out earlier that the component titles are not intended to stand for any kind of psychological entity: for 'factors', 'forces', 'mechanisms', 'innate abilities' or anything else of that kind. When we score S for 'having' or 'lacking' PHIL, EMP, etc. we are simply answering questions of the general form 'Is it true of S that . . .?' We are not answering any questions about *why* this is true or untrue, about what mechanisms or forces make it true or untrue. This is quite a different enterprise, no less important, but one which (in my view) it would be hard to undertake successfully unless and until our present enterprise is successfully concluded. In other words, until we know the answers to the general question 'Is it true of S that . . .?', I do not see that we have much chance of propounding clear and plausible hypotheses about the underlying causes, for we shall not even have clearly identified the phenomena we want to explain.

This needs stressing, because empirical research lives in a world densely populated by various entities or 'constructs'. I am thinking here not only of such terms as 'social class', 'ego-strength', 'super-ego', etc., but of words seemingly more relevant to our present interests—'ability', 'capacity', 'competence', 'motivation', 'attainment' and so on. I confess to extreme confusion about the meaning of such words as used by empirical researchers, confusion perhaps not unshared by the researchers themselves. Nevertheless, there will be a standing temptation (to which I as well as others may succumb) to describe our components by the use of such terms. The temptation is hard to resist, because at least some of them (for instance, 'ability') are normal English words, and would be the most natural terms to use in certain descriptions.

In what immediately follows I want to clarify the status of each component in terms of the question 'Is it true of S that . . .?'. If I can do this, we need not become entangled in the undergrowth of quasi-technical terms, nor ambiguously specify this component as an 'attainment', or that as an 'ability', or the other as a 'motivational factor'. To put this another way: on the one hand, we need to be absolutely clear about what we are testing for under the heading of each component. We must be able to say of any evidence that turns up in our assessment 'This is (is not) part of *what we mean by* "having PHIL" (EMP, GIG, etc.)'. On the other hand, we must steer clear of thinking that there is some underlying *thing* for which we are testing—as if our assessment was only valid if it got at this underlying thing. We are concerned with what PHIL, EMP, etc. are by definition. ( I shall consider this point again when discussing validity in the next section.)

PHIL(HC)     If S has the concept of a person, then S *can do* certain things (most obviously, identify—once he knows the facts—certain instances as falling under the concept). There is no question of S's *wanting* ('being motivated') to do this, or of S's being the sort of person who, with time and teaching, may get to be able to do it ('innate ability'? 'potential'?). S has simply got to be able to do it, at the time of assessment, *if* he wants to or is induced to.

PHIL(CC)     If S claims the concept as his overriding moral principle, and thinks that he ought to use others' interests as the criterion of decision and action, then this is simply something that S *does*. We are not concerned with cases where S *cannot* do this owing to some preventing factor outside S's control (for instance, S is under hypnosis or threatened at gun-point or drugged). So we are concerned with what S *does when he can*. (We shall be careful, however, to interpret 'he can' in a wide sense to include S's unconscious desires, beliefs and emotions.) The context of assessment must be one in which S *can do what he wants:* we then assess what S actually does.

PHIL(RSF-DO) & (RSF-PO)

If S has DO and/or PO feelings, then again he simply *has* them. There is no question of his being able to have them, or wanting to have them (though again we must be sure that they are *his* feelings, that is, feelings which arise out of his perception and thinking, not feelings induced against his will).

Feelings (in the present sense of emotions, not sensations) are logically made up of characteristic beliefs, symptoms, and tendencies to action. (This was discussed more fully under EMP.) Thus an S who evinces the DO feeling of remorse will believe he has done wrong, show symptoms of guilt, and perhaps tend to apologise or make restitution: and so with other DO and PO feelings. Verification of these three elements is required if it is to be true of S that he feels X or Y, and the verification will vary with the particular feeling.

EMP(HC)

This is analogous to PHIL(HC), in that we are here concerned only with whether S has the concepts of various emotions (moods, feelings, 'states of mind', etc.). It has to be true of S that he can, if he wants, bring certain phenomena— beliefs, symptoms, actions, circumstances—under the same criterion. The criterion would normally be represented by a word—'jealousy', 'pride', etc.—and full knowledge of the meaning of such words would be a sufficient condition for S's having the concept. (But not a necessary condition: he may have the concept under some other heading.) Whether S can in practice, or in practice wants to, identify particular emotions is not in question.

EMP(1)(Cs)
EMP(1)(Ucs)
EMP(2)(Cs)
EMP(2)(Ucs)

All these are concerned with whether S *can, in practice,* identify emotions: that is, whether he can recognize and correlate the various evidences of emotion in himself and others, in respect of conscious and unconscious emotions. They are not concerned with whether S actually *does* do

|  | this; for S may not want or be induced to do it, yet still be able to do it. Lack of incentive is lack of KRAT(1): we are here interested in the presence or absence of ability. |
| GIG(1)(KF) | Both of these are concerned with whether S |
| GIG(1)(KS) | does actually know relevant facts and sources for relevant facts. No sense is to be attributed to saying 'Does S *want* to know?'. Some sense may be attributed to saying 'Does S want to *remember* the facts?': but we are not concerned with *why* S knows or does not know, only with whether S actually has the knowledge (can consistently produce the right answers for his own or others' benefit). |
| GIG(2)(VC) | These are components of 'knowing how', and |
| GIG(2)(NVC) | may fairly be called 'skills'. S must be good at (skilled in, competent at) behaving in certain ways, verbally and non-verbally. Neither propositional knowledge ('knowing that') nor motivation are here in question. |
| KRAT(1)(RA) | These again are all things which S does or does |
| KRAT(1)(TT) | not do. Is it true that S attends relevantly (RA) |
| KRAT(1)(OPU) | to real-life situations? That he attends and thinks thoroughly about them (TT)? That he ends up by making an overriding, prescriptive and universalized decision to take action (OPU)? Here too S must be able to do these things: we are not concerned with cases in which some external compulsion prevents him. |
| KRAT(2) | Here we need to know only whether S in fact carries out his decision: again, provided he could carry it out, and not permitting situations of compulsion. |

We may now be able, perhaps without too much risk of confusion, to categorize these components under various headings that may be useful to empirical researchers. I shall eschew (and would advise the reader to eschew) such terms as 'cognitive', 'affective' and 'motivational'. But it may help to give a quick sketch under three headings, as follows:

*A. Knowing*
The following components seem to be concerned with different kinds of knowing:

| PHIL(HC) | knowing what counts as a person. |
| EMP(HC) | knowing what counts as anger, jealousy, etc. |

EMP(1)(Cs)
EMP(1)(Ucs)  $\Big\}$ knowing when X feels anger, jealousy, etc.
EMP(2)(Cs)
EMP(2)(Ucs)

GIG(1)(KF)  $\Big\}$ knowing that some drugs are addictive, etc.
GIG(1)(KS)

GIG(2)(VC)  $\Big\}$ knowing how to apologise, welcome, etc.
GIG(2)(NVC)

## B. *Doing*

| PHIL(CC) | what S does here is to *claim* the others'-interests rule as his moral principle. |
| KRAT(1)(RA) | what S does is to notice, to be relevantly alert. |
| KRAT(1)(TT) | what S does is to think thoroughly. |
| KRAT(1)(OPU) | what S does is to make a 'proper' decision to act. |
| KRAT(2) | what S does is to take action. |

## C. *Feeling*

PHIL(RSF)
(DO & PO)

having a feeling (emotion) is, as we saw when discussing EMP, partly to have a *belief*, and partly to have a tendency to *act*: so that to this extent we are dealing with something that S *does*. Nevertheless certain *symptoms* are also conceptually required, and are from some viewpoints the central aspect of emotions: so this merits a separate heading. Emotions, we might say, are neither things we know nor things we do, but things we suffer (or that happen to us).

# 6. Reliability and validity

I put under this general heading certain considerations which assessors need to bear in mind if the assessments are to be effective. 'Reliability' and 'validity' are supposed to be basic concepts in psychometry, but I suspect they are often vague, and some of these considerations might come equally under either title. So I shall simply list the considerations in order. I shall naturally omit certain standard points connected with statistics, correlations, and other technical if important details of test-design: for I take these to be well-known to competent researchers, and (at least in most cases) not to present any conceptual problems.

## 1. In what way must the assessment be valid?

The assessments we are concerned with here are sufficiently different from much psychological testing and assessment to merit explanation. Many tests are, in a strong sense, *predictive*. That is, they claim that if S does such-and-such (scores 130 on an IQ test) he will, or will be in some degree likely to, do so-and-so (pass an examination, earn more than £2000 a year, make a good airline pilot). Some predictors seem to have a close causal connection with what is predicted (IQ and examination success); others seem not to have (height and university entrance); others again are uncertain (going to a British 'public school' and 'doing well' in the world). But all these tests are concerned with predicting X from Y *where Y is not part of what is meant by X*. Such tests, and the empirical correlations and co-variances they show, are interesting and important, but they are not directly relevant to our purpose here.

This is because what we are out to test for is a good deal more obscure than passing an examination, or earning £2000 a year, or entering a university. It can be easily verified whether S does these things, and hence easily determined whether a test successfully predicts that he will do them; but elsewhere this does not hold. If we are interested in *what we would normally mean by* 'morally educated', 'a happy marriage', 'mentally healthy'—or even such terms as 'intelligence'—then we have a prior and quite different problem.[1] We have the problem of how to assess, or verify, *when it is the case that* S is morally educated, or happily married, or mentally healthy. We may first work out, as I have done elsewhere, what is meant by these phrases; but we still have to work out how, in practice, to verify that they apply to S. Obviously, this can be done well or badly. If we tried to verify happy marriages by counting up the number of times each partner called the other 'darling', we should be doing it badly, for this assessment, though easy, bears little relation to the normal meaning of 'a happy marriage'.

The validity of our assessments, then, consists simply in whether they give us a representative sample, a 'fair slice', of whatever it is we are trying to get at. In this sense they are exactly parallel to at least one function of examinations at schools and universities. A teacher wants to know how good a student is at mathematics: he sets a number of typical or representative problems and finds out. If the teacher sets a test in order to find out whether the student will pass an examination in the future, he is doing something quite different. Here his test may be representative of the problems likely to be set in the future examination, but it need not be. He might simply rely on available tests (if any) of the pupils' intelligence and willingness to work hard, and use those to predict their success or failure. Prediction is, in this case, his sole concern.

There is of course a weak sense in which our tests, or any other tests that we may call 'representative' or 'sample' tests, are supposed to predict. That is, if they are any good, they have to be 'fair slices' of S's performance, and this means that one can predict that *other* slices of S's performance will be roughly similar. This is, naturally, not a matter of taking a *random* sample of S's thought or behaviour, but of taking a *fair* sample, or an *average* sample. We can only determine whether our sample is fair by taking a great many samples in different contexts and under different conditions— like taking many samples of river-water to determine the silt-content.

We may, of course, look ahead at the possibility of other tests of a different kind. Once we can *identify* Ses as having PHIL, EMP, etc. —and this is, inevitably, our first task as empirical researchers—we may want to go further in several directions. First, we may want to devise shorter, more easily administerable and scorable *predictive* tests: that is, tests which will enable us to predict (without the

1. IME, Ch. 4: PER, section 3.

bother of assessing it directly by representative samples) whether S would, if directly assessed, turn out to have PHIL, EMP, etc. Secondly, when we have our representative tests, and also some idea of the psychosocial factors which allow Ses to acquire the moral components, we may be able to devise tests which will tell us whether S is likely (under certain standard conditions) to acquire these components (S's 'innate potential' or 'capacity' to become morally educated). Thirdly, we may devise tests of schools and other institutions which will enable us to predict how far these institutions are likely to encourage or discourage S's acquisition of the components; and so on.

However, I do not think we should be in too much of a hurry to do this. The great defect in much psychological and sociological research has always been the misplaced desire to have 'hard', quantifiable, data, together with definite and preferably statistical 'results'. Moral education does not lend itself to this treatment (and, I would add, neither do many other topics concerned with human intentional behaviour). For the purposes of moral education, at least, our second priority after the sample tests should lie in the direction of before-and-after studies, studies with matched groups, and longitudinal studies—our purpose being primarily to determine what can be *done*, in schools and elsewhere, to increase the components in various Ses, in such a way that the increases stay with them for life.

## 2. Consistency and naivety

Many tests require to be 'reliable' in the sense that Ses are supposed to give approximately similar responses (gain similar scores) on different occasions. Our assessments raise somewhat different problems. First, if S gives predominantly (say) PHIL(CC)-type answers on Monday, but different answers on Tuesday, this will not mean that our test is necessarily unreliable. It may mean that this, in fact, is a correct picture of S's thinking: on Monday he feels well-disposed towards his fellow-men, on Tuesday he has different feelings. This point is likely to apply still more strongly to changes of *context* (rather than time): it is well known that a person is likely to think and act in one way when alone, in another when with a group of friends, a third when with his parents or teacher, a fourth when in committee, and so on. It would be odd if this were not so: we should expect some inconsistency, and try to cater for it by varying the times and contexts of our assessment.

This raises a problem about what S 'really' thinks. Consider the assessment for PHIL(CC) again. S1, we will suppose, gives the answers which he thinks the tester (or his teacher or someone else) expects from him. But this implies that he has available, and could produce, his 'real' beliefs, and we can in principle (and to some degree in practice) organize the assessment-context so that he will in fact give the 'real', and not the expected, answers. S2 also gives answers pleasing to the teacher or assessor or parent, but in his case because he really thinks that these are the *right* answers: the answers represent his actual beliefs and principles, even though they may be founded upon authority-obeying reasons. We have no problem here either, for these are his real principles; the fact that he has acquired these principles from teachers or parents is irrelevant—they are now *his*. S3, however, is such a fluid person that he seems to have no consistent views of his own at all: he will say what is expected or what he thinks is expected, and if you then ask him what his own, real beliefs are, he just looks blank. (I here describe a by no means uncommon case.)

This is a problem, because if we now ask of S3 'Is it true that he claims the concept of others' interests as his overriding moral principle?', we can only reply that he claims this no more, and no less, than any other principle: he *has no* principles, he is wholly inconsistent. Of course, in his actual decisions and behaviour (if he is human at all he is bound to decide and act sometimes), he will have to follow some overriding syllogism—to do *something* for *some* reason. So for other components our problem is at least mitigated; but for PHIL(CC) it exists. All we can do, I think, is to note for all Ses the amount of consistency of principle. I say 'all we can do', but to be able to assess for this is itself to have gained a great deal which is both interesting and important for moral education.

Secondly, there is a difficulty about 'test-sophistication' not wholly disconnected from the problem mentioned above. To take our extreme case (S3), who begins by saying the first thing that comes into his head or what he thinks will make us testers happy, if we now say 'Yes, but what do *you really* think? Should you use principle A or principle B, for instance?', and so on, then we may be creating in him, perhaps for the first time, a genuine opinion. We say 'Is it A or B?', and S3 may never have even distinguished between A and B (let alone subscribed to one of them). All this may be excellent as a method of moral education, but not as a method of assessment. We shall have to allow for an inevitable tendency to destroy Ses' original naivety.

## 3. Sincerity and rationalization

I have suggested elsewhere (and other writers have dealt with this area more fully) that one reason why there has been very little effective research in this area is because empirical researchers have failed to grasp, or at least to cater for, the characteristics of rational (rule-following, intentional, language-governed) behaviour. Briefly, in this area we have to be concerned with 'what goes on in S's head': with S's reasons, intentions, and purposes: with what S says or could say to himself and to others. This area is covered neither by S's overt behaviour, nor by S's 'attitudes'. Much work has been done on both of these, but its relevance to our interests is uncertain. Hence there exists, not so much a 'gap to be filled' in research, but a whole new dimension of research which clamours for our attention.

I shall leave aside difficulties attaching to particular components, and take the hardest case as an illustration. The morally educated S acts in others' interests, but this simple-sounding phrase includes a great deal. S must not only have or claim others' interests as a principle [PHIL(CC)], he must also apply it or bring it to bear [KRAT(1)], together with EMP and GIG, so as to produce [with KRAT(2)] the right (other-considering) action. It would not be enough for us to establish (1) that S had the principle, nor (2) that S produced an other-considering action, nor even (3) that S had the principle *and* produced an other-considering action. We have to establish that S acts rightly *because* he has and applies the principle. It is what comes into the sense of 'because' here that causes our research difficulties.

Part of the sense of 'because' is that S *follows a rule*, or acts for a reason: that S has the principle in mind and intentionally uses or applies it (as opposed to S's happening to act in accordance with it for some *other* reason). The normal method of verifying such cases is by what S says, or could say; we simply *ask* S 'Why did you give him money?', and S replies 'He needed it' or, more fully, 'When people need things, I have a rule that I should give them what they need, and that's the rule I followed'. If S, whatever his verbal incompetence, could sincerely say nothing of this kind, even given time and encouragement to express himself, we should doubt whether he had followed a rule at all. This does not, of course, imply that S must have gone through a conscious process of ratiocination at the time of rule-following: all of us every day follow rules without thinking about them. But it is the way in which we distinguish rational action from reasonless, impulsive or compulsive be-

1. IME, Ch. 4: PER, Part I.

haviour. Most human behaviour is, in this sense, rational; indeed, we might not want to call it 'human behaviour' if it were not.

But another part of the sense of 'because' is that S's rule-following must be the *cause* (not just the reason) for S's action. It must be *operative* in the world. It must be the case that S's reasons *produced* S's action, that they were not just left in the air, so to speak. This too we take to be true of much, if not most, of human behaviour: human beings characteristically carry out their intentions, and do in action follow the rules which they follow in thought. When S says to himself (or could say if asked) 'I will move my pawn to this square, in order to save my queen', following a rule or rules which justify this reasoning, S will characteristically move the pawn: and so with other actions. If this general principle did not hold good, a great many human activities (not only chess) would be impossible. The normal method of verifying this part of the 'because' consists in observing whether S's reasons are, in point of fact, followed by the appropriate behaviour on the part of S. Here we do not only ask S, but observe what S does.

To assess effectively for both parts of the 'because' requires complex and subtle techniques. Suppose we put S in a situation, in which others' interests are involved and he has a choice of decision and/or action. Then (to repeat) we need to know *both* that S brought a PHIL-type principle to bear on the situation—that S said to himself, as it were, 'I must satisfy others' interests in this case'—*and* that this bringing-to-bear of the rule was causally effective, resulting in action. We need then to employ, for the same situation, *both* the verification-methods which consist basically of asking S (finding out 'what is going on in his head') *and* the verification-methods which consist of correlating that with the subsequent action. All this needs to be fitted into our scheme of components, and will be discussed in more practical detail when we come to consider actual assessments for KRAT(1) and KRAT(2).

It may well be thought that this area is so fraught with difficulty as to present insuperable problems for the practical researcher (whose position, after all, is in some respects less favoured than that of the clinical psychologist). In reply I would say two things. First, if we are to be concerned with the area of rule-following and intentions at all, the problems simply *are there* and must be tackled. It is not so much that they are insuperable as that few empirical researchers have paid them sufficient attention. I am not for a moment suggesting that what I have written here actually solves any practical problems: only that it sets the stage for practical solutions. Secondly, a more practical point. In our list of components, we have distinguished KRAT(1) from KRAT(2) in such a way that most of the unconscious factors are taken care of—one might say, swept under the carpet—under the heading of KRAT(2). For S will have KRAT(1) if he makes only a *decision* (reaches the DIK-stage). True, the decision must be sincere: but, as explained elsewhere, we shall not press 'sincere' beyond what it normally bears. The decision must be, so to speak, consciously sincere. If there are unconscious forces or 'syllogisms' that make him *act* otherwise, we shall say that he lacks KRAT(2). It will, I think, be found considerably easier to get effective assessments of sincere decisions (even of overriding and prescriptive sincere decisions) than to try for more. Briefly, we may induce lack of KRAT(2) by measuring the decision-action gap. This in itself will get us a long way, even if we cannot say very much about the *kind* of lack of KRAT(2) which operates for particular Ses.

## 4. Criterion groups

A standard method of ensuring that tests are valid is to take groups of people who should (if they *are* valid) perform very well or very badly on the tests. If we are testing for X, and know that group A has lots of X and group B very little then we can confidently expect that, if our test is any good, group A will do well and B badly. All this is well known. How far does it apply to our assessments?

This is a question which could only be answered in full by considering it in relation to each of the components in turn. But one's first reaction ought, I think, to be one of suspicion. For the question arises 'Is it the case (for any or all of the components) that we can identify such groups by other criteria *which are more reliable than the assessments themselves?*' In general, the answer to this seems to be 'No'. But there may be exceptions, and it is worth a brief discussion.

First, we must avoid two obvious errors. (1) We must not select criterion groups suggested to us by tradition or partisan values. For instance, it would be absurd to use 'saints of the Christian church' or 'moral heroes of today', because it is not clear that these people are paradigms of the morally educated person, though they may be paradigms of what is admired by a particular creed or culture. Similarly the criminals or juvenile delinquents of a particular country no doubt lack *something*: but what they lack may be merely the intelligence not to get caught, or the willingness to fall in with an oppressive régime. (2) We must resist the temptation to think globally (as one might think in terms of 'villains' and 'heroes'). It is fairly useless to choose groups who consist of what we take to be 'virtuous men' and 'wicked people'. Members of both of these groups may well have very different scores on the different components (Iago may have had less PHIL, but certainly had more EMP than Othello).

The real trouble is that, although each of us could no doubt list a number of people who (we would confidently assert) would score highly on any good test of some particular component, these people are not easy to identify publicly. I may know, or think that I know, that A is a firm believer in others' interests, B a very 'aware' or 'insightful' person, C very alert to moral situations, and D a man of such determination and wholeheartedness that he always carries out his decisions. It would perhaps not be absurd to form a criterion group from people known to researchers or others *who were thoroughly clear about the components*: this would at least be an improvement on allowing those who were *not* clear to select a criterion group on some 'global' basis ('good men', 'saints', etc.). This might be worth doing: but I would be as suspicious of my own judgement as of other people's, and, in any case, there seems to be no easy, quick way of identifying such a group by public criteria rather than personal acquaintance.

There may be exceptions to this; but I am not sure how convincing they are. One might argue that a criterion group of moral philosophers ought to score more highly on PHIL(HC)—having the concept of a person—than other people would (and the naive might believe that moral philosophers would score more highly on other components as well); or that philosophers of mind, if anybody, would be likely to do well on EMP(HC)—having the concepts of various emotions. Winners of quiz programmes or 'general knowledge' tests might be better at GIG(1); and the 'social skills' of GIG(2) might be thought to emerge clearly in youth leaders and air hostesses. Slightly more seriously, it would be nice to suppose that 'trained psychotherapists' (if such a group could be clearly demarcated) had more insight and awareness of their own and others' emotions, and hence were better at EMP(1) and (2). Can we say that those in positions of pastoral responsibility have more alertness to moral situations [KRAT(1)(RA)], or that we can define a class of 'mentally healthy' or 'integrated', 'conflict-free' individuals whose KRAT(2) is at a high level? All this, or some of it, may not be silly: but it is not obviously sensible either.

It is somewhat more plausible, I would guess, to take criterion groups for various *areas* of behaviour of thought to which the components apply (like the areas mentioned under PHIL(CC) and relevant also to other components). We might be better able to identify Ses of whom we could at least say that they had high PHIL(CC) as regards money (or sex, or democratic voting-procedures), and other Ses whom we knew had low PHIL(CC) as regards, say, interaction with coloured people, or punctuality. These could be used as high or low criterion groups for testing in those areas; and this is far from worthless.

In general, I should like to leave this question wide open. It may be that, by the mere process of *trying* to get criterion groups, we shall learn a great deal that will be of use for assessment. What we must not do, in my view, is simply to assume that a certain group is a criterion group. There may be arguments for using certain groups that are more watertight than any I have considered above; and I do not want to preclude this. Like many other matters, this is something that must be left to individual researchers: I have only tried to warn them of certain dangers.

### 5. 'Variables': longitudinal and other studies

One difficulty which psychometrically-orientated researchers may have with assessment stems from a long tradition associated with words like 'variables', 'factors', etc. I cannot discuss this tradition here, and in any case the points that need to be made do not require it. First, our assessments are *not* concerned with establishing *why* S performs well or badly in respect of any component, only with *whether* and to what extent he does. Secondly, we are for this reason unworried if good performance correlates highly with social class, or IQ or other 'variables'. For we are not trying to test for something which is *empirically* distinct from (say) IQ, only for something which is *logically* distinct. It may well be that whatever makes S intelligent also makes him a good performer.

This does not mean that we need have no concern at all about such 'variables'. If, for instance, *only* Ses with high IQs perform well on a 'story'-type test, we might suspect that the wording of the story was too sophisticated for low-IQ Ses to understand it. Tests and assessments can be *unfair* in this way. But all that we have to be sure about is that the assessments do actually assess the components, and not something else: that S's performance would normally be taken, on straightforward, logical grounds, as good (if partial) evidence that S did 'have' the component. Further questions about *why* S 'has' it must be left to a later stage of research.

The only 'variables' with which the assessor need be seriously concerned are to be found in the components themselves. This is why it is so important to distinguish them logically, and in the test-forms. We need to be sure that it is (say) S's PHIL, not his GIG, that we are assessing. So we must hold the other components constant when we are assessing each one. Of course there will be other requirements to ensure that the test is 'fair': perhaps the most important of these is the *context* in which it is taken.[1] But these I must leave to the (more experienced) empirical researcher.

This does not mean that the researcher ought not (nor that he ought) to see how far our assessments correlate with other things. When he reaches the further stage of trying to give some causal account of what produces the components in various Ses, of course, he will have to do this. But we may find it convenient to look at correlations in the course of this first stage; and certainly the results could be interesting. For instance, suppose we develop adequate assessments for PHIL and KRAT, it would then be interesting to see whether Ses who performed well were also rated as 'helpful' or 'responsible' by their teachers; whether they ever committed crimes; whether they reached certain social positions, and so on. (Assessment of various 'leader'-figures, such as senators, members of Parliament, etc. might prove particularly exciting.) But we must keep these other enquiries distinct from the basic assessments.

Rather more interesting, in my view, if our concern is to prepare the ground for serious causal hypotheses, would be to determine the correlations between our components and certain general capacities which seem to be connected with them. These connections would be various: some logical, some empirical. For instance,[2] the ability and/or willingness to *discuss* things efficiently with other people—and by 'efficiently' I refer to such things as listening to others, not being hostile, etc.—might be thought either a case of possessing certain components, or at least a strong indicator of possessing them. Other indicators might be roughly described as 'being able to take a joke against oneself', 'self-esteem', and so on. Many of these may themselves be hard to assess; but they are likely to be more relevant than some (not all) of the easy-to-get, easy-to-quantify data, such as the crime statistics.

One 'variable' with which the researcher will need to be concerned fairly soon, however, is age. The 'normative' researcher or moral educator is, after all, interested in what produces morally educated *adults:* the hypothesis that Ses do not change in respect of their moral components after the age of (say) 18 is, to say the least, unsupported. We should therefore require, at some early

1. See pp. 61–2.
2. IME, pp. 201–02.

stage, longitudinal studies assessing different age-groups. (I mention this partly because the practical form of assessments should not, for this reason, only suit children or adolescents.) What ages we should assess would depend on our views about what factors are likely to operate: thus it is not so much the mere passage of time, but (I would guess) major psychological events such as having a job and earning money, marriage and having a family, etc. Probably we should begin by assessing up to the age of (say) 30–35, not beyond.

In the whole of this area much will naturally depend on the researcher's particular interests, and I am not sure whether there is much point in my saying what I think those interests *ought* to be. If one's brief is 'moral education in the secondary school', then naturally this title will readily suggest the sort of correlations which one will be interested in establishing in the course of the basic assessments. If one has a topic-title, like 'race prejudice', this suggests other things; if 'juvenile delinquency', other things again; and so on. The most important point, however, is to keep one's other interests from sneaking into the assessment-process itself: it is chiefly to make this point that I have discussed some of these 'other interests' here.

# 7. Strategy and forms of assessment

## A. Strategy

Few serious people working in this area would deny its remarkable complexity. But it is possible to react to this complexity in different ways—some sensible, some less so. My intention here is to distinguish the former from the latter, in the process of considering the various forms of assessment required.

For assessment of anything that can respectably be called 'moral education', our criteria for the morally educated person must be non-partisan and 'culture-free'. I have explained this point *ad nauseam* elsewhere, and will take it as read. The next point to grasp is that 'global' or all-embracing criteria, cast in such general terms as 'maturity', 'sense of responsibility', etc., are too vague and wholesale to be of much use. This too I will take as read; but it has important consequences. Once we start breaking down the criteria into detail, into our individual components, we at once perceive the immensity of our task. It is here that the less sensible reactions tend to occur, with which I now want to deal.

First, it is important not to renege on the basic point. We may be tempted to say something like 'Look, we can't possibly assess each of these many components in turn: it would take ages, and we're pressed for time. So what we will do is to lump at least some of them together: we'll try to assess in some general way for PHIL— never mind about the distinctions between PHIL(C), PHIL(CC) and PHIL(RSF). Or perhaps we'll assess generally for "good moral thinking" on the one hand, and then for "good moral action" on the other'. I do not say this temptation should never be yielded to. Political, economic or other practical pressures on particular research teams may make it inevitable. But *if* it is yielded to, the researcher must be as careful as possible to collate the components intelligently. For instance, it would not be absurd to devise some generalized assessment for EMP as a whole, rather than for the five sub-components we have listed; to collapse PHIL(HC) and PHIL

(CC); and so on. But it would be evidently absurd to make other collations—say, of EMP with KRAT. It may be that test scores will show high correlations between different components; but this has to be *shown* before we can collapse them, even for practical purposes, and, of course, the logical differences between them still remain.

Another, worse, way of reneging is to abandon the assessment of components altogether, and to concentrate on assessment of *topics*. Here political and other pressures are likely to be still greater. Topics like 'race prejudice', 'social class barriers', 'delinquency' and others become fashionable. The cry goes up that something must be done about it, and so of course it must. But it is apparent that those topics are only, so to speak, practical slices or cross-sections cut from the components (like the areas in which PHIL may operate, mentioned on pp. 45–6). *In* the area of race relations, or sex, or social class, or whatever, various Ses will have or lack one or more of the components, and the only really safe and effective way of educating people in these areas is to discover which components they lack, and how to develop them. Of course, if we are not so much interested in education as merely in preventing certain phenomena (race riots, drug-taking, etc.) by *any* means, that is a different matter: important, but not for the *educational* researcher.[1] From the latter's point of view (which is not the politician's) topics are subordinate to the components.

We may also conduct what might be called 'research', but should at best be termed 'research-and-development', without making any serious attempts to assess for the components. This involves making various (more or less intelligent) guesses about factors in education which are likely to inhibit moral education, or contribute to it. For example, we may be inclined to believe that many teachers overplay a certain role (usually labelled 'authoritarian'), and devise materials and methods designed to combat this—free discussion, the 'neutral chairmanship' of the teacher, and so forth. Or, *per contra*, we might guess that too many teachers were too 'permissive' in the discipline they exercised, and try to persuade them to enforce certain specified sets of rules and sanctions. If these guesses are clear and sensible, much good may be done. The trouble is that they are not usually even clear (as perhaps the above two examples show); and, in any case, any serious assessment of their merits would take us back to the components again.

1. PER, section 8.

A much more satisfactory strategy—I incline to think, both for 'practical' and political as well as for 'research' interests—would be to employ the more obviously logical method of tackling the assessment problem piecemeal. Thus we might begin by taking one component—say, PHIL(HC)—and ensure first that we had satisfactory assessments for this; and then move on to another component, and so forth. Here we should not only resist any temptation to collapse components together, but should be on the look-out for further distinctions which may have escaped the present writer or other writers. We should be out to make quite sure that we have covered all the ground, and broken it down into as much logical detail as possible: and then go over it bit by bit. There is no need here to say more about this aspect of strategy; I merely wish to stress its evident merits for anyone who is at all serious about the subject.

Secondly, the wide variety of assessments needed demands a particular type of strategy. It will already be evident that we are here concerned with far more than one particular form of assessment or test. The components are such that pencil-and-paper tests, interviews, check-lists, behavioural observation, practical experiment, simulation-situations and many other forms are required. More importantly, the *cumulative* nature of the components necessitates that many of these forms be applied *to the same Ses*. We need to know, for the same S, that he has the concept of a person, *and* claims it as his moral principle, *and* brings it to bear when making decisions, *and* acts on it. Not only the conceptual links between the components, but also the presence or absence of each in respect of S's decisions and actions, requires study of the same Ses by various methods.

I do not say that this applies to all components. For instance, in the case of what we may call the purely 'cognitive' components— PHIL(HC), EMP(HC), and GIG(1)(KF and KS)—it would be possible, and useful, to devise tests which could be applied to children or other Ses without there being any particularly close contact between assessor and assessed—just as we can ʳassess children for having certain concepts in mathematics, or knowing certain facts in history. It would also be possible to assess for some other components—the various forms of EMP(1) and (2), and GIG(2)— independently of the rest, although here we should be unlikely to succeed at all with pencil-and-paper tests, and so would require closer contact and participation. But for what we may be tempted to call the central components—PHIL (CC), PHIL(RSF), various forms of KRAT(1), and KRAT(2)—

it is clear that we need to get at the same Ses in various ways.

This means that any researchers concerned with this area will be likely to need groups of Ses who can be studied, under different conditions, over a long time period. Some of these studies might be done in a 'laboratory' situation, where Ses can be observed in action, interviewed before, during and after acting, given pencil-and-paper tests, made to role-play and engage in simulation studies, and so forth. Or it may be possible, for instance, to study Ses in one or two particular schools, in depth and intensively. I do not want to go further in details of practical suggestions here: but obviously the picture required is—one might say—much more like that of the anthropologist, or the participatory social psychologist, and less like that of the quantifying sociologist.

Thirdly, something depends on our ultimate interests. If we are concerned with moral education in a somewhat restricted way— that is, with what can in practice be done in schools and other educational institutions to improve Ses' moral components—then I would suggest that we should not be too anxious, in the first instance, to cast our net over a very large number of institutions and societies. We may use small sample groups of Ses (representative of what we take to be the significant factors—as perhaps social class, religious commitment, etc.) and ensure first of all that our assessments are adequate. Armed with these, we may conduct before-and-after studies to see if this or that method of moral education affects their components; or, of course, we may use matched (but still small) groups. We should hope to find methods that would be effective for very large numbers of Ses. This is, naturally, a different matter from trying to determine what factors *in general* are responsible for having or lacking the components: our interest here is chiefly in what can be done, in schools and other such institutions, to improve them.

Finally, so far as general strategy is concerned, I would stress the need for close co-ordination of research, and for clear conceptual understanding on the part of researchers. Much research that is conducted under such mysterious titles as 'socialization', 'learning to live', 'personality development', 'moral development and many others may be very valuable. Since, however, I am not convinced that very much of it is founded on a clear conceptual basis, I am not sure of its relevance to moral education as we have described it. If it is relevant, then the findings have to be looked at in the light of the components (and I have given some examples of this earlier in this book). The point is not that researchers should not pursue their own interests: only that those interests must be *clear*.

## B. Forms

In the next section I shall attempt the dangerous task of suggesting specific forms of practical assessment which seem to fit each component individually, but before this I want to list all the possible forms of assessment that might be relevant. This will at least show the wide variety of choice which we have, and if my later suggestions are misguided, researchers will be able to draw on this bank for other attempts. To experienced researchers, much of this section may seem obvious or naive. But I think it important not to take too much for granted.

I shall make no attempt to categorize these forms. It might be possible to do so, though different criteria would produce different categories. Many psychometric textbooks make use of various category titles, but I have found them more confusing than helpful. So I shall simply list, with brief explanations, various forms of assessment that might be used, without reference, of course, either to their (practical or theoretical) advantages or drawbacks. Nor shall I here be concerned with problems of scoring or quantifying the assessments.

1. The pencil-and-paper 'questionnaire' form: this to include tests which might not strictly count as questionnaires, such as Osgood's semantic differential test.

2. The pencil-and-paper 'story' form, or 'case study', in which S is asked questions after the story. This may vary in different ways, particularly in whether S is asked (2a) questions with yes-or-no answers, or to rate on a five-point or some similar scale, or (2b) open-ended questions.

3. As above, with stories orally given.

4. As above, with the stories visually given. By this I mean that the stories are 'told'—that is, enacted—on film, or by real-life actors, or puppets.

5. 'Free composition' by S, after initial stimulus-material (e.g. we say to S 'Write an essay about your vices' or 'Tell us what's wrong with your school'). This may vary according to the medium: (5a) pencil-and-paper, (5b) oral, (5c) acted or otherwise visually represented (perhaps drawn or painted) by S.

6. 'Interviews' (a grand name for asking S informal questions). These may be more or less formalized ('structured'). More important for our purposes is whether they are conducted (6a) before, (6b) during, and/or (6c) after S's deciding, or doing, something.

7. Reportage of others of S's performance in respect of various components. This may again be formalized or structured (we ask

someone to fill in the items on a questionnaire or check-list), or more informal. We may distinguish the following 'others': (7a) teachers or other authority-figures, (7b) close friends of S of his own age, (7c) those who know S well, excluding the two previous groups, (7d) S's family, excluding the previous groups, (7e) any who could plausibly count as 'experts' (e.g. a clinical psychiatrist).

8. 'Hard' facts about S given from other sources. This would include, for instance, S's record as a juvenile delinquent, whether S turns up punctually to class, and so on.

9. Contrived observed behaviour. The researcher here induces S and perhaps others to do something (involving more than verbal responses), and observes the result. This might be categorized according to how strictly 'experimental' the set-up is. Here I shall distinguish various kinds of things S may be asked to do: (9a) act or role-play, (9b) take part in a group task, (9c) perform an individual task, (9d) deal with a 'presented situation' (e.g. the researcher arranges for an old lady to fall down in a teen-age coffee bar).

10. 'Free' observed behaviour. The researcher here simply observes slices of uncontrived behaviour: e.g. how S acts in the football ground, when crossing the road, in the lunch queue, when he has the chance to cheat, and so on.

11. Informal self-reporting. Here I refer to methods by which S speaks or writes about 'what is doing on in his head', without the need for an interviewer, before/during/after S's behaviour. For instance, S might be trained to give a 'running commentary', which could be taped, on his thoughts and feelings. This method may be unfamiliar to some researchers, but seems to me of great potential value for our purposes.

12. Existing tests. I add these even though it is not at all clear which existing tests are relevant to which components (if to any). But there are at least some cases where such tests seem sufficiently relevant—perhaps to a combination of components—to be well worth applying: for instance, Feffer's 'decentering' tests seem relevant to EMP.

To begin the task of relating the above forms of assessment to the moral components, we can divide the components into three groups:

*Group A* is not concerned with 'in the field' action or ability, but with qualities we might call 'cognitive' or 'theoretical'. This group includes PHIL(HC), EMP(HC), PHIL(CC), and GIG(1)(KF & KS).

*Group B* is concerned with 'in the field' abilities and skills, and includes EMP(1)(Cs) and (Ucs), EMP(2)(Cs) and (Ucs), and GIG(2)(VC & NVC).

*Group C* is concerned with action, decision-making and feeling 'in the field', and includes PHIL(RSF) (DO & PO), KRAT(1) (RA, TT & OPU), and KRAT(2).

The relevance of this division is as follows. We cannot get at the components in Group C—not, at least, with any certainty—unless we have first assessed the components in Groups A and B *for the same Ses*: apart from other reasons, some of the components in Group C involve S's making use of components in the other groups. (Thus KRAT(1)(TT) involves bringing to bear S's EMP, GIG, etc., and the assessor must first know that S *has* some EMP, etc. He might be able to induce this from the whole KRAT-situation, so to speak, but it would be risky.) On the other hand, we can assess Group A independently, and Group B independently: the only possible muddle here would be trying to test for EMP(1) and (2) before testing for EMP(HC).

I mention this, then, not only because the three groups differ in nature and (as we shall see) can be assigned different assessment-methods *a priori*, but also because it will affect researchers' practical strategy. It would be possible to deal with Group A and stop there: to deal with Group B and stop there. Of course, this is to leave out the whole 'motivation' and 'action' side of morality: but it would still be useful in its own right. Many researchers may not have the resources to do more. Those that have, or who use their slender resources to concentrate on a very few Ses but take in all three groups, need to remember that Group C cannot be looked into on its own. There is already a great deal of research on 'moral behaviour' or 'behaviour' more generally (delinquency, etc.) which unfortunately tells us little about S's *morality*, precisely because it has not been combined with assessment in Groups A and B (as well as for other reasons).

We now need a scheme linking assessment-forms with particular components. The numbers in what follows refer to the forms mentioned a few paragraphs earlier. I have put them under two headings, 'probable' and 'possible'. This represents a guess—quite possibly mistaken—about which forms are likely to be the most successful. About this, and about what follows generally, researchers must make up their own minds.

| *Group A* | *Probable* | *Possible* |
|---|---|---|
| PHIL(HC), PHIL(CC), | 2(a,b),3,5(a,b), | 4,1,5(c),12. |
| EMP(HC), GIG(1) | 6(a,b,c) | |

*Group B*

| | | |
|---|---|---|
| EMP(1)(Cs & Ucs) | 2,3,6(a,b,c),7(e), | 1,4,7(a,b,c,d),9(c), |
| EMP(2)(Cs & Ucs) | 9(a,b,d),11 | 12. |
| GIG(2) | 7(e),9(a,c,d),10 | 7(a,b,c,d),12. |

*Group C*

| | | |
|---|---|---|
| PHIL(RSF) | 4,6,7(b,c,e),9(a,b, d),10,11 | 1,2,3,5,7(a,d),12. |
| KRAT(1) | 6,7,9,10,11 | 1,2,3,4,5,8,12. |
| KRAT(2) | 7,8,9,10 | 1,2,3,4,5,6,11,12. |

I commend this schema to researchers, even though they may prefer their own ideas to the sketches which follow. A few additional notes must be made:

1. Numbers without qualification include all sub-forms: e.g. '6' means '6(a,b,c)'.

2. I have not taken into account here (nor will I later, since this is best left to individual researchers) such things as S's reading ability, IQ, age, and *some* other things that may affect the *practical* form of the test or assessment. Nevertheless the *general* forms here suggested are, I think, applicable in principle to almost all age and IQ groups, with due allowance made. Some of these forms will have no merit, of course, unless certain practical conditions are established: I deal with some of these in the following section, but only where I think that the points may not already be standard practice for competent psychometrists.

3. It is also obvious that the question of whether or not a particular form fits a component depends on *how* it is used. For instance, I have listed 2 (the pencil-and-paper 'story' form) as only a 'possible' for KRAT(1) and (2). But if this form is used for self-reporting on actual *behaviour* it may be very valuable.

4. As will become apparent when we consider the sketches of assessment, especially for KRAT(1) and (2), the possible use of certain techniques (one-way screens, contrived 'temptation'-situations, 'planted' observers, etc.) raises moral problems for the researchers themselves. I will not deal with these here: but the techniques are so important that I have tried to say something about them in an Appendix.[1]

---

1. Appendix I.

# 8. Sketches of assessment

## Group A

*PHIL(HC)*

One might think that one could get at PHIL(HC) in the course of assessing PHIL(CC), PHIL(RSF), KRAT(1) and KRAT(2). Ses that *claim* and *use* the concept of 'other people' (in the required sense) must of course *have* it. But Ses that do not claim or use it may do so either because they do not have it, or for quite other reasons, and this difference is important. Moreover, it will be very difficult when assessing PHIL(CC) and KRAT to be sure that it is precisely *this* concept that S claims and uses, and not some apparently similar concept. From a practical (educational) viewpoint, also, it is important that S acts for what really are the right reasons—briefly, 'other people' for S must not be white, biped, etc. but rational creatures who are sources of needs.

The kind of question we need to put (in some suitable form) to S is: 'Is there anything which A,B,C, etc. all have in common?' (where A, B and C are 'persons'). We check S's concept by varying the other characteristics of A, B and C: thus we make one black, another looking like a dog or a robot but with the mind of a man, another with tentacles, another looking like a man but actually a robot or zombie. Or we could ask: 'If you were distributing goods (votes, rights, food, living-space) to various entities, what would you want to know about them?'[1] We then present S with various possible criteria of similarity—size, colour, shape, English-speaking, niceness, eating the same food, made of flesh, etc. Or we say that someone else is distributing goods, and picks entities A, B and C but not D, E and F; we tell S lots of things about A–F, and ask him why the distributor picked the ones he did.

Again: 'You catch something on Mars and put it into a zoo. There is a rule that you mustn't put people in zoos, but the rule

---

1. In this case we assume that S wants to use the PHIL-rule. Such assumptions have to be checked by assessing PHIL(CC), if there is any doubt at all.

doesn't say what counts as "people". What would you want to know about the thing you've caught?' Or we reverse the story with a Martian catching earth-things. Useful for our purposes here will be *borderline* or *worrying* cases, e.g. embryos (shape but not rationality), parrots (talk but not rationality), and possible Martians. (Science fiction is a good quarry for the assessor in this respect.) Are dolphins 'people'? It will be surprising if very many Ses (at least above a certain age) fail to count people with different shapes, languages or skin-colours as 'people' in our sense, since they look more or less alike. We have to probe S's concept by harder cases.

This obviously fits the 'story' form (2): but open-ended questions (2b) are likely to be more useful than yes/no replies, or scales (2a). Oral stories will be important, since it may be hard to get our questions into words that all Ses will easily grasp (3). Free composition (5) will be useful as an extension of the open-ended questions. Most important of all will be the interviews (6), conducted certainly after the 'story' test (6c) but also during (6b) and possibly also before (6a). The merits of an easily-scored test would chiefly depend on the results of such interviews, conducted of course by an assessor who has a clear grasp of the concept himself (given which, I doubt if assessors would differ very much after sufficient informal conversation with the child).

I should not hope to get very much from 'visual' methods, but it might be useful to 'tell the story' for non-verbal children in dramatic form (using puppets, etc.) (4). Straight questionnaires and grids *may* turn out to be useful, and could be tried; their correlations with the methods already mentioned would be interesting (1). I doubt if much would be gained by (5c) acted or otherwise visually represented 'free composition'.

In assessing PHIL(HC) we have of course to hold constant S's *'recognition'*-abilities[1] and any other irrelevant factors. In our terms, these will be EMP and GIG. This should not be too difficult. Naturally we also need to ensure that S has a fair chance to show that he has the concept: we must not hurry him or make him anxious, although we must give him sufficient incentive. I leave these problems to the researcher.

### PHIL(CC)

The most important requirement here is the production of *conflict*-situations. At present, we can only guess at the most likely 'overriding syllogisms' that may operate for Ses (even at the level

1. See p. 42.

of their 'moral theory', which is what we are concerned with here,
let alone the level of practical decision and action). But the various
'modes' elucidated by Williams[1] may be useful here. These can be
easily cashed out, with a little imagination, into particular 'pulls'—
peer group pressure, being rewarded, feeling guilty, and so on.
Other 'pulls' within these categories can be produced to cover the
various areas in which Ses may perform differently:[2] thus we can
ask S what he thinks he ought to do 'when someone you don't
know asks for (needs?) help', 'when someone you don't like asks for
help', '. . . who doesn't like you', 'who has "done you down" ',
and so on. I shall not try to cover all the areas here, because there
are too many.

Stories, written or oral (2,3), will obviously be an appropriate
form here, but many of the questions should be open-ended (2b),
and they need to be supported by informal interviews (6), chiefly
after S's completion of the story-test (6c). The 'free composition'
assessment would be a convenient cross-check (5), besides giving S
more leisure to think. For non-verbal children an initial stimulus
by visually-presented material might be useful (4). The questionnaire form and grid-form may turn out to correlate well with other
forms, but should not be used as a starting-point (1).

There are enough story-suggestions available for me to have no
need to create more here. More important is that our questions
should satisfy OPU requirements. We have to ask S (in some form),
after the story: (1) 'What ought you to do?', (2) 'Why?', (3) 'Do
you think that it really is the most important thing to do, more
important than anything else?', (4) 'Do you think that *you* really
ought to do it, not just that *somebody* should', (5) 'Do you think
anyone else in the same position ought to do the same?', (6) 'Would
you feel sorry/guilty afterwards if you didn't do it?' (or, 'Would it
matter much to you if you didn't do it?'). We could also present
the story, and ask S to say what *elements* in it he thinks he ought to
consider (i.e. others'-interests elements, self-considering elements,
and so on).

Stories should be given both in first-person and in third-person
form: so too with interviews. With the third-person form, there
seems little point in asking S what he thinks the story-person *would*
do. But with the first-person form this may be very useful. My guess
is that it would be best to keep the 'ought' and the 'would' as
distinct as possible. (First, we ask S what he thinks he ought to do,

1. Williams (1969, 1970).
2. See pp. 45–6.

making sure of the OPU requirements; then we say something like 'Now turn over', and on the other side of the paper 'You've said what you think you ought to do. Now we want to know what you think you *would actually* do, whether right or wrong', and so on.) We must also ask S *why* he thinks he would do it, if only to make sure he has got the distinction clear. If this fails, it may be necessary to clarify it for him by a prior informal interview.

It is quite possible that the stories we invent are not perceived as conflict-cases by some or many Ses. This is why interviews are essential. We need to 'put Ses on the spot', so to speak, making the various conflicts as obvious as possible. Indeed, in scoring such assessments, apart from a possible necessity to give various scores for the various areas, we should pay most attention to what we may call the *tenacity* of S's adherence (if he adheres at all) to a rule about others' interests.

We must remember that we are not here concerned with 'self-sacrifice' or 'altruism' in any sense of those words which would require that S treated himself as *less* important than any other 'person'. Stories concerning voting situations, 'fair distribution' situations, etc. should be able to elicit those Ses who are (at least on paper) 'self-sacrificial' in this way. They should not be marked down for this, so long as their reason really concerns others' interests, and they are not just following codes of 'good manners', 'ideals of self 'sacrifice', etc. By arranging stories and situations involving greater, equal and less need on the part of others this should become reasonably clear.

'Free composition' might be given in the form of asking S to write an essay on some situation where others' interests were involved (another conflict-situation), or perhaps we get S to say who he thinks to be the 'best' (most virtuous, moral, etc.) person he knows, and then ask him how he thinks this person would handle a conflict-situation. This might be profitably acted out (5c), as well as written. S can also be asked to grade historical or imaginary people who have followed this or that rule, or to grade parents who brought up their children to follow this or that rule.

Care has to be taken (as we saw earlier[1]) over what the words 'ought', etc. mean to Ses: and I should be inclined to check this independently, either by interview or by other methods. We might ring the changes on 'ought', 'right', 'good' and their opposites. We could ask Ses, 'When you say you ought to do X, do you mean (i) your parents/friends would expect you to? (ii) it would be the

1. pp. 15–18.

most profitable thing to do? (iii) you have been told to do it by teachers?', and so on.

Assessments for PHIL(CC) must of course be correlated closely with those for KRAT(1) and (2), for reasons given elsewhere:[1] of particular interest will be Ses' remarks on what they *would* do, and why, if this is not the same as what they think they ought to do. It may be that, for the sake of KRAT assessment, we should extend our inquiries here, to see if we can discover (from S's self-reporting) whether he would even get to the decision-stage (DIK) ('Would you decide to do it but then not have the nerve, or would you not even get as far as deciding?'). But this turns on the (unknown) merits of self-reporting.

*EMP(HC)*

Here I think assessors will need to put in a good deal of preliminary work, in the form of general observation of Ses' spoken and written words, and interviews (6). For it seems almost inconceivable that any S could *not* have the concept of at least certain basic emotions and moods—for instance, fear, hope, anger, misery, joy, etc.[2] On the other hand, some Ses may not have the concepts of the more sophisticated or 'belief-laden' emotions, such as (perhaps) remorse, pity or pride. There is much work to be done here, philosophically as well as empirically—the two should go hand in hand.

However, that Ses will inevitably have *felt* X or Y does not mean that they necessarily have the *concepts* X or Y. Consider this extract from a tape-recording:

'Do you know what fear is?'
'Yes, it's when I have a sort of funny trembly feeling inside.'
'Don't you have that when you're angry too?'
'Well, it's different somehow.'
'Do you want to run away when you're angry?'
'No.'
'What sorts of things make you frightened?'
'Thing that give me the trembly feeling.'
'Dangerous things?'
'Yes, no, well, things I don't like.'
'Do other people feel frightened?'
'Yes.'
'How do you know?'
'Well, I suppose they're like me.'

1. pp. 58–60.
2. IME, p. 121.

'Do you mean they have a trembly feeling, or they run away?'
'No—well, I don't know.'

It seems to me possible (and not just from this sort of evidence) that Ses may have *a* concept of fear, anger, etc. but not 'our' concept. By 'our', I mean the concept described earlier under EMP,[1] which brings under the same criterion of similarity the various features of (i) characteristic or necessary belief, (ii) involuntary symptoms, (iii) behaviour, and (iv) typical surrounding circumstances. In particular, Ses may have one concept for their own fear, and another for other people's. Assessments, then, will attempt to see how good Ses are at correlating (i)–(iv), and at inducing one feature from others.

For EMP(HC), as against EMP(1) and (2), we are interested in S's ability to do this 'at leisure', so to speak, rather than 'in the field'. Specific 'recognition'-ability is not in question. The story-form, therefore (2 and 3), is suitable. We present S with a story-situation, giving him some or all of the features (i)–(iv), and asking him to induce others or give the constellation of features a name (jealousy, fear, etc.). ('Mary is in a field and a bull chases her. What does she feel? What will she want to do?'; 'John loves his mother but she spends all her time with his brother James. What does John feel? What goes on in his mind?'; 'Molly is trembling all over and clenching her fists. What does she feel?', and so on.)

As these (over-simple) illustrations show, there may be more than one 'right answer' to our questions (Molly may be frightened or angry); we might present S with a list of possible answers, two or three of which could be right, others of which are certainly wrong. We can also use 'visual' presentations (4) of symptoms, postures, and gestures characteristic of various emotions; but we must be careful here not to make the presentation such that S will be carried away by the *story*—that verges too much on EMP(1) and (2). We may, however, for instance, show pictures of facial expressions, or stylized cartoons of situations. All this has to be supported by informal interviews (6); free composition (5a,b) and the open-ended questions (2b) are an extension, probably useful.

*GIG*(1)(*KF & KS*)
This is the easiest of the components to assess, since it is a matter of straightforward, factual knowledge. We can here be brief.

1. pp. 51–2.

The only difficult with KF is to ensure that the 'hard' facts *are* likely to be relevant for the assessed Ses. (Facts about the addictive properties of obscure garden-grown drugs would not have been immediately relevant for Ses in 1930, but arguably they are for at least some Ses today.) However, under your three headings[1] of (i) health, safety, etc., (ii) laws, norms and conventions, (iii) individuals or groups in need, it will not be too hard to include central and permanently relevant facts. Cigarettes and other drugs, road safety, first aid, elementary biology, contraception and venereal disease, hygiene; the criminal and civil law, traffic regulations, standard social expectations in human and group interaction, conventions of dress, privacy, etc., local politics, school rules (for pupil-Ses); facts about old people, the underprivileged, the mentally ill, and so on—these are some of the areas one would naturally think of.

KS may be assessed independently (e.g. 'Somebody offers you a cigarette and says it contains cannabis. You are not sure whether cannabis is a dangerous drug. Who would be the best person to ask: a friend, a teacher, a doctor, your parents, the local chemist?'); or it may be better to combine it with KF ('Your boy friend wants to sleep with you and says that there is no chance of your getting pregnant, even if you don't use contraceptives, provided you only do it on certain days. (i) Is this true or false? (ii) If you're not sure, would you ask another girl, a doctor, a clergyman, a teacher, your mother, another boy?').

The 'story'—(virtually, the 'examination')—form will be appropriate here, written or oral (2,3). Free composition, e.g. essays showing grasp of relevant facts or oral accounts (5a,b) may well be of more use than interviews (6). The 'possibles' in this area hardly seem worth using [unless we count the questionnaire form (1) as an examination-form].

## Group B

*EMP*(1)(*Cs & Ucs*)
*EMP*(2)(*Cs & Ucs*)

I shall deal with these together to begin with. They are among the hardest to assess. The chief methodological point to bear in mind is this: we are not out to assess whether Ses *have the concept* of various emotions—that is EMP(HC)—and we shall have to hold that constant in assessing EMP(1) and (2). [Hence we shall have to use

1. pp. 56.

the same Ses for EMP(1) and (2) as we have used for EMP(HC).]
But nor are we out to assess only for S's *using* his ability to identify
his own emotions and others' 'in the field'—that is KRAT(1),
which we shall also have to hold constant. We must have 'in the
field' situations, but not situations in which S is distracted, made
anxious, subject to various emotional 'pulls' himself, and so on.

This is not too difficult to do with EMP(2), because we can put S
in situations where he is not emotionally involved. But it is difficult
with EMP(1), because here S is concerned with his own emotions,
which may themselves be distracting [KRAT(1)] factors. Thus it
may be that an angry S *can* identify his own anger all right (EMP(1)
(Cs) ), and can even recognize that underlying this anger he has
a feeling of insecurity or being threatened [EMP(1)(Ucs)]: but
he just does not want to bring this identification-ability to bear
[KRAT(1)]—he is too busy being angry, so to speak.

However, there are (obvious) ways round this. For EMP(1),
we can again use the written or oral story (2 and 3) ('You are in the
following situation . . . what do you feel?'), along lines suggested
when considering EMP(HC) earlier. But better, because nearer to
'in the field' situations, will be visual presentations (4). We show S,
on film, himself and others interacting, and ask him to identify the
various emotions displayed at different times. By skilfully arranging
the film or story, we can see how far S can correlate beliefs, symptoms, actions and surrounding circumstances. And these methods
will, of course, work for EMP(2) also.

Yet it is one thing to watch oneself on film, and another thing to
'watch' oneself in 'real life'. The distinction between motivation
and ability [KRAT(1) and EMP(1)] is very hard to draw here;
but it seems fair to say that many Ses will be better than many
others at being *able* (rather than willing) to identify their own
emotions in virtue of, or despite, the fact that they are 'standing in
their own shoes' rather than watching themselves on film or TV.
Some Ses are simply better at self-interpretation than others. So
we have to check this out by putting S in a 'real-life' situation in
which his emotions naturally emerge: by interviews (6) or, questioning at just the right moment, we stop him and say 'Right, what do
you feel now?' Or we get him to write down what he feels in some
form of 'self-reporting' (11). This will be a (naive-sounding) attempt
to keep KRAT(1) constant.

Naturally, we can ask him at some time *afterwards* what he felt
(6c), when the distracting KRAT(1) factors will be less powerful,
and this is certainly worth doing. But *eo ipso* we shall be further
away from assessing S's ability to say *at the time* what he feels. If we

could devise an effective 'running commentary' form of self-reporting it would be very useful, for KRAT(1) as well as for EMP(1). We can, however, put S into these contrived situations (9) with some hope of success. There will be some occasions when it will be obvious that S knows he feels (say) angry, and is deliberately controlling himself, and many other occasions on which informal questioning will produce results.

For EMP(1)(Ucs) we should have to rely, not only on these methods, but on the judgement of trained psychologists or psychotherapists, who could (for this particular purpose) count as 'experts' (7e). Those close to S in some capacity (7b,c,d) may also be helpful. Nor should this help be spurned for EMP(1)(Cs). EMP(1) is very hard to test; and the best procedure will probably be to use the suggestions just made, together with any others that seem to fit the concept, and see how they correlate.

EMP(2) is easier, because we do not have the KRAT(1) distractions; or we need not, if we plan sensibly. We put S behind one-way screens, etc. so that his own emotions are not involved. We make him role-play (9a)—perhaps a particularly fruitful method. Remembering our interest in S's ability to imagine, as well as directly observe, what others' emotions are, we can give him story-situations where a 'stretch of the imagination' is called for. We can score Ses, if we will, not only for performance in the different areas,[1] but on a general dimension of 'immediacy-remoteness' (unless of course we count this as an 'area').

### GIG(2)(VC & NVC)
The chief difficulty here is to hold the other components constant. For plainly S's competence, in practical situations of verbal and non-verbal communication, will depend to a great extent on his awareness of others' feelings [EMP(2)], his factual knowledge about them [GIG(1)], and his bringing-to-bear of these [KRAT(1)]. Yet the 'practice' or 'skill' element is also important. Assessments for GIG(2), therefore, must be undertaken hand-in-hand with assessment of the same Ses for these other components.

Obvious methods for this are role-play (9a) and other forms of contrived observed behaviour (9c,d). 'Free' observed behaviour (10) may help the assessor to distinguish between the particular 'skill' element and the effect of various KRAT-'pulls'. Since there is some solid research in this area, we could hope for a lot from assessment by 'experts' (7e); and it is even possible that these experts could

1. See p. 46.

provide us with general categories known to be relevant—e.g. the eye-movements, postures, distance between S and others, forms of social ritual, etc. Conceivably S might be given scores for these various categories, if we knew that good performance in them was tantamount to competence at GIG(2).

The two main lists we should require for assessment would be (1) a list of what I can only call 'social acts': for instance, welcoming, giving orders, apologizing, encouraging, thanking, criticising, etc.; and (2) a list of social contexts, e.g. at a party with friends, in a foreign country, meeting strangers, interviewing or being inter- viewed, in committee, and so on. (Of course these lists overlap.) I should be inclined to form a consolidated list from these two areas on the (pragmatic) basis of what 'social acts' and social contexts S will be most likely to *need* this component for. Most of them are common to all cultures and societies and there should not be too much difficulty in agreeing on the list. It may well be that GIG(2) is not 'situation-specific', for the most part; everyday observation at least suggests that some Ses are better than others, in general, at 'cottoning on' to the required social ritual or 'game'.

## Group C

*PHIL(RSF)(DO & PO)*

PHIL(RSF), it will be remembered, is an 'in the field' component, like all the components in this group. Whilst it may be useful to assess S's feelings in 'remote' contexts [e.g. when presented with a story (2,3)], or to see how far S's 'self-reporting' of these feelings in such contexts is valid, our chief concern will be with 'real life' situations. S's self-reporting *when engaged* on these, however (11), may be a most important method.

'Direct' assessment of S's feelings can only be obtained by asking S, and trying to ensure an honest answer (6). Indirect assessment is by observing S's symptoms and actions in contrived (9) or real (10) situations. The respective merits of each will turn largely on practical difficulties; but it is worth pointing out that inductions from symp- toms and actions can be easily misleading, and if we can overcome problems of insincerity I should expect more from the 'direct' assessment.

Further, it may be found desirable to put S into situations where he cannot or need not act on his feelings—that is, to keep KRAT(1) and (2) out of the way. Here all we would have to go on is what S says, plus any very obvious symptoms: and the former may often be much better evidence. It is in this light that we ought to see the possible merits of visually-presented stories or situations (4). Keeping KRAT(1) and (2) out of the way may also help to ensure that S's RSF are not lost without trace beneath other more powerful feelings that may arise if S is called on to act and decide.

The type of situations is derived from the notion of PHIL, as explained earlier. The fact that we may sometimes want S to participate (decide and act), and sometimes not, may force us to make a rough distinction between feelings like *remorse* (if we so contrive it that S acts mistakenly and harms others), and feelings like *pity* (where no action is required of S at all). We need to ensure that the feelings are genuinely 'rule-supporting' by questioning S about the *criteria* of actions to which the feelings prompt him or from which they arise. (E.g., does S feel prompted to give clamouring or pathetic children *whatever* they ask for, even when not in their interests? Does he feel remorse even when he has done the right, PHIL-type, thing? Does he feel sympathetic towards others in that he earnestly desires their good, or is he just 'sentimental'? The assessor needs to find practical methods of determining such questions: I do not pretend it will be easy.)

The DO/PO distinction will also be hard to operate. But it should be possible to identify Ses who are not only rule-governed (PHIL-governed) but who have some sort of emotional investment in the rule as such: whose pleasure lies in having followed the rule more than in having done some *good to others*. A lot has been written on the 'psychopathic' personality, to whom other people are 'not real'. From a study of this and of psychological literature on emotional attachment and 'identification' generally the researcher may discover what signs to look for and what questions to ask. Feelings of *grief* and *sorrow* are particularly relevant to the PO area, of *remorse*, *disapproval*, and what many Ses will call 'conscience', to the DO.

Good practical assessments here turn on getting good situations which will also be effective for KRAT(1) and (2). We will now consider these, remembering their relevance for PHIL(RSF).

### KRAT(1) and (2)
I remind the reader (i) that we have to keep PHIL, EMP and GIG constant; (ii) that our concern here is not just with overt behaviour. Consequently (i) the same Ses must be used; (ii) the decision-and-action situations we employ must lend themselves to interviewing (6) or other reason-getting techniques.

We may expect something from the self-reporting asked for in PHIL(CC) tests (2); and 'hard' facts from outside sources (e.g.

about S's punctuality, honesty, and other overt behaviour) will be a useful check on assessment—particularly if the facts *are* 'hard', and we do not ask vaguely after S's 'reputation' or standing in the eyes of teachers and others, but for specific observations (7,8). 'Free composition' (5) may perhaps be expected to reveal something also. But most is to be expected from free or contrived observation.

One experimental method might be to get S to play some game in which he has the chance to profit unfairly from others (e.g. by having learned to toss a coin so that he can make it come down whichever way he likes), or to win by doing others down. This might work provided we keep the incentive constant, which is hard, particularly in an experimental situation. But in a 'laboratory'-type situation it may be that Ses (perhaps particularly young Ses) will get sufficiently carried away by the game for the counter-PHIL motivation not to be too artificial or fluctuating. Similarly, to allow for other 'pulls', we might place S in experimental situations where all the 'other people' were advocating that he behave in a non-PHIL way. Tightly-controlled situations of this kind lend themselves to more precision of assessment: but artificiality is a severe disadvantage.

More profit, I think, is to be expected from contrived situations (9), and 'free' observation (10). In choosing between these, the assessor will need to determine how many 'free' situations there are which are observable, and which will give him what he wants. Behaviour in games-playing, in the playground, in the dinner queue, at the football stadium, in certain coffee-bars, etc. may perhaps be relied on to generate the right context: with a little trouble, the assessor would certainly find some 'free' areas which he can use both for observation and for interview (6). He may improve his observations by cameras, hidden tape-recorders, one-way screens, and so forth.

He will certainly be tempted, however, to make use of a device which might be thought to raise moral problems. As I think that these can in principle be overcome,[1] I will consider it here. He can get Q-men[2] (or children) to act as spies, possibly even as *agents provocateurs:* that is, to create and/or report on situations which the assessor might otherwise find it hard to observe. Q-men could be old ladies asking for help, a girl who appears to steal another girl's boy-friend, a boy who acts as a tempting target for bullying, a boy who acts unjustly or unpleasantly, a teacher who behaves

1. See Appendix I.
2. Borrowed from Q-ships (armed merchant ships disguised as unarmed, to lure and sink submarines) in World War I.

nastily but then needs help, a child who is lost, Pakistanis in areas
where the youths are racially prejudiced, ugly and pretty girls
needing help, and so on. The researcher's imagination will no
doubt outstrip my own in devising situations with the assistance of
Q-men: there are in fact very few situations which could not be
thus set up.

The 'areas' here will correspond both to the PHIL areas and the
KRAT(1) areas mentioned earlier. Thus we arrange, above all, for
different 'pulls' (the peer group, authority, guilt, etc.), also for
contexts of sharing goods or powers, of harming rather than
helping, of different kinds of 'others', and so on. We arrange situations of repaying debts, taking advantage of others' weakness,
letting others down, stealing, etc. Much may be gained in a general
way (and some existing research here may be relevant) by observing
the role S plays in interaction with others when there is no specific
temptation-situation. Does he take the lead autocratically, hang
back, display 'democratic' leadership, try to go by the general will,
or what? The assessor may observe this without moral misgivings.

Crucial, but difficult, is the timing of the interview-questions (6).
I should be inclined to let S act in his own way, apparently un-
observed, in the same type of situation to begin with, let the assessor
cull what he can from external observation, and then let him apply
his questions suddenly just before what he takes to be the decision-
point, or just after (but before the actual behaviour). Reportage by
Ses much after the event may be contaminated by all sorts of factors;
and the sort of self-monitoring suggested in 11 is itself contaminating,
insofar as (if S is properly trained in it) KRAT(1) is thereby
increased—S is already more attentive, alert, thoughtful, etc.

Questions will be of the form designed to elicit RA, TT and OPU.
'How did you see this situation?', 'What description did you give
to yourself of the Pakistani before you hit him?', are the type
relevant to RA. 'What did you think he'd feel?', 'Did you realize
that the car might swerve?', relevant to TT. 'What did you decide/
are you now deciding to do?', 'Did you say "I ought to do X"?',
relevant to OPU (with necessary additions, some of which might be
satisfactorily gained from assessments of PHIL beforehand).
Getting clear and useful answers to such (here highly generalized)
questions will depend on ingenuity in setting up the original situation.

Despite the distinction made between KRAT(1) and KRAT(2),
I willingly grant that *one* very good way of checking for KRAT(1)
is to see what S actually *does*. This is certainly the easiest (some might
argue the only safe) way of checking for O and P. This method must

restrict itself to those (very many) cases where there is unlikely to be any strong counter-motivation: that is, where it is very unlikely that S prescribes to himself and commits himself without action following. This would exclude, for instance, situations of addiction or classical 'neurotic' situations. If we exclude these, the method is a good one.

How far we can, in practice, merge KRAT(2) with KRAT(1) must depend on the efficacy of our methods. If we can get clear evidence of sincere OPU decisions independently of actual behaviour, this will be immensely useful: and we then write off those cases where behaviour does not follow to KRAT(2)-deficiency. In those (not infrequent) cases where the decision precedes the behaviour by a significant time-span, the distinction is important. (Here existing research on 'deferred gratification', 'impulse-control', 'ego-strength', etc. may be relevant.) One's suspicion is that sincere decisions get *lost*, very often, when the passage of time allows the intervention of some other overriding syllogism, and the extent to which this is true of various Ses is extremely important.

It is clear that the components 'culminate' in KRAT(1) and (2): and that if we are interested in moral behaviour at all (or indeed in *prescriptive* moral thinking), these components are perhaps the most important of all. I should hence be inclined to consider the KRAT area in terms of what situations, contexts, areas and experiments may conveniently be used, and tailor the 'stories' and other methods to fit these. There is not much point in testing for PHIL(HC) and (CC) in an area which we cannot hope to use for KRAT, or, at least, the point is severely limited.

## Conclusion

I hope in the foregoing section to have given sufficient indications, at least, of the way in which the practical development of tests and assessment methods ought to proceed. These suggestions, as I have stressed, are both fragmentary and tentative; but whatever their merits and demerits, they should in any case serve to remind us of some important points of procedure, which I should like to emphasize before concluding:

1. First and most important, it will be clear that in this field there is no precise 'cut-off point' at which 'the philosopher' can retire, and 'the psychologist' or 'the psychometrist' can take over. There are, indeed, certain initial considerations which are almost entirely conceptual or philosophical: and there will be tasks in test-development—although arising at a much later stage than we have reached

in this book—which may be safely hived off to the statistician or the strictly 'behavioural' scientist. But there is an enormous middle ground, to map which the researcher requires both philosophical and psychological ability. I have argued elsewhere[1] that this is true of much psychological research, and that it needs a closely co-ordinated team of researchers—or, at the very least, researchers who are aware of the nature of the problems and hence able and willing to deploy the necessary expertises. A sharp distinction between conceptual and empirical problems is not possible here.[2]

2. It follows that we can expect progress by two main routes:

(a) There is a great deal of psychological data, particularly in the post-Piagetian tradition, which needs analysis and reworking. Although (as I have tried to show in Part I) nearly all of it is conceptually naive and not to be taken at face value, it is still extremely important; and if it were handled by researchers with conceptual as well as empirical competence, it might have far more to tell us than it now can. In particular, much of the data might usefully be fitted into the scheme of moral components outlined in Part II, thereby filling out the very thin and skeletal picture we have so far.

(b) At the same time, we need adequate research teams, of the kind described in 1 above, to pursue the business of assessment along the lines and conceptual framework which I have tried to show to be necessary. With a very few exceptions, these do not exist at present.[3] Such teams would not, I think, need to spend a great deal of their time in analysing or building on the work of past researchers, for as I have argued, there is not much that is really solid on which to build.[4] They would be better employed in main-taining conceptual and methodological clarity at all costs, and (in a sense) starting from scratch.

3. Finally, we must not expect quick results. The whole area requires much more care, and much more clarity, than researchers have yet devoted to it. Only sustained, imaginative and precise thinking over a long period of time will enable us to make the progress which the importance of the subject merits.

1. PER, Chs. 5 and 11.
2. ibid., Ch. 4.
3. The Warborough Research Unit at the Oxford Dept. of Educational Studies, and the Ontario Institute of Studies in Education, are two honourable exceptions.
4. See Appendix C.

# Appendix A
## Moral difficulties with research techniques

To deal with this topic properly would be to go deeply into practical moral philosophy, which I cannot do here. What I can perhaps do is to make some points which bear upon the techniques suggested in the 'sketches of assessment' (Part II, 8), which might reasonably influence researchers in one way or another.

1. First, it need hardly be said that there is a good deal of opposition, not to say instinctive prejudice, on the part of the general public and perhaps particularly those in charge of educational institutions, to any research into 'morality'.[1] This is over and above their objections that research is time-consuming and a nuisance for them. (The mere word 'morality' conjures up various fantasies and the researcher may well prefer not to use it.) Some of these objections may be well-founded, others may not. This is merely to make the point that the researcher will inevitably meet with what might be called 'political' difficulties on the part of others, as well as with moral difficulties himself. They are connected, however, because the more the researcher becomes known to and trusted by Ses and those in charge of Ses, the more likely he is to be able to overcome the moral difficulties. He must from the first regard himself as a participator and (so far as possible) helper, not just as an observer.

2. The 'moral difficulties' of research can easily be exaggerated: views tend to be doctrinaire and to suggest a 'keep-one's-hands-clean' attitude. We must distinguish, from genuine moral difficulties, not only the political difficulties mentioned above, but also any need the researcher may have to preserve a good 'image' in the eyes of the public; in other words, he may need not only not to do

---

1. Quite an interesting piece of research might be done to establish correlations between those people/institutions who are loudest in their demands that something should be done to 'improve moral standards', 'prevent delinquency', etc. and those who actually welcome research in practice. I suspect an inverse correlation.

wrong, but not to be thought (even by idiots) to do wrong. There are limits to this principle, which has to be balanced against the importance of the actual work: if one was always governed by what others thought, one would do little or nothing. But the principle is a real one.

3. Setting these points aside, however, we need to remember that we do not always, as researchers, have a duty to *help* Ses in particular situations, nor even a duty to do nothing which makes life more difficult for them. If this were so, most kinds of tests and assessments would be impossible. Instead of allowing the S to make mistakes in his Latin grammar test, one would help him towards the right answers: indeed one would not 'make life more difficult' for S by setting the test at all. Instead of observing children crossing the street, in an endeavour to determine what method of instruction encourages children in general to cross safely, the researcher would be at the kerb-side helping them.

It does not seem clear to me that moral assessment is different in kind. We are perhaps apt to think that it is, because it seems mon-strous that the assessor should encourage—or even observe—Ses to do 'something bad', 'a sinful action' etc. Certain kinds of experi-ments, it might seem to us, are 'putting temptation in S's way'. We might claim this of the various 'cheating' experiments, or of experiments encouraging Ses to administer electric shocks to other Ses. But what does this amount to? If I ask S for the genitive singular of 'dominus', 'campus', and a string of other words (all of which end in -i), ending with 'opus' (of which the genitive is 'operis'), am I 'putting temptation in his way'? Surely I am, in just the same sense. The temptation is not moral temptation, but why does this make a difference? Because moral temptation is more 'serious'? But S might stay awake all night wondering whether he has got the genitive of 'opus' right, just as he might wonder about whether he should have cheated or administered shocks. Of course, one might conclude from this that one should conduct neither test, but this does not differentiate moral assessment *per se*.

In *Oliver Twist*, Oliver is in a sense 'tested' (with very poor controls) by his benevolent patron: will he take the books honestly, or will he run off with them? (In fact he gets caught by Bill and Nancy and forcibly brought back to Fagin, thereby rendering the test invalid.) Is this objectionable? Certainly, if the effect of the 'temptation' was very serious and long-term—if, for instance, it had encouraged Oliver to return to a life of crime—then we might fairly object. This would be rather like the researcher encouraging Ses to take addictive drugs. But this is hardly in question. Is it objectionable because the thing is contrived—the 'benevolent patron' *used* the situation *as* a test?

I think there is something in this point: our normal relationships with, and expectations of, other human beings preclude the tester-testee relationship, unless it is specially catered for. The researcher seems, as it were, to be taking unfair advantage of these normal relationships for his own purposes. In the extreme case, if spies or Q-men are used,[1] or perhaps as in the Milgram experiments, the researcher seems monstrously parasitic on normal conditions of trust and privacy, rather as (other) dishonest people—liars, thieves, and so on—are parasitic on standard norms of honesty.

4. This 'breach-of-trust' point seems to me more serious, and more difficult to deal with, than the 'putting-temptation-in-S's-way' point. The latter can, I think, be got over by firm rules about anonymity. Provided it is true, and Ses are convinced, that nothing that they do will be held against them, or will be recorded in any form such that it could conceivably be used against them, many Ses will be content. It still seems important, though, that they *should* be content: for to some Ses the mere fact that somebody *knows* what they did is hurtful. It might be arranged that even the researchers did not know what individual Ses did what. This could be done if we were assessing a whole group, such as a class of children, without taking the individuals' names. But in general the question seems to turn on whether Ses agree to assessment, whether it is *voluntary*.

If it is voluntary, only a doctrinaire person could sustain the 'breach-of-trust' point. To give an example which I hope will cover several points at once: suppose various Ses wish to be diplomats or commandos or something of the kind. We have to be sure that they are able to resist certain temptation-situations, not always rely on the loyalty of those around them, and so on. So we say to the Ses: 'Look, if you want this sort of job you will appreciate that we have to put you through a training and assessment course which will check these qualities. You may not find it pleasant.' Then, if they agree, we can see no moral difficulty.

Provided this move is made, and that Ses give us a fair mandate to assess, I do not think the researcher need worry too much. Nor need he be prevented, by his role as assessor, from also being a participator and a friend. One author says, criticising the view 'that it is the duty of a social worker to establish a relationship of friendship with her clients; but that she must never forget that her first

1. See p. 99.

duty is to the policy of the agency by which she is employed', that this is a 'debasement of the notion of friendship as it has been understood, which has excluded this sort of divided loyalty, not to say double-dealing.[1] But if one could not have friendship and trust where there were also other (perhaps prior) loyalties, e.g. to one's country or one's wife, then there would hardly be any friendship at all. What produces 'debasement' or 'double-dealing' is not the existence of other loyalties or interests, but some form of *cheating* which Ses have not allowed to the researcher in a mandate.

5. The position is complicated in the case of children or those 'in care' or 'under charge'. When considering similar problems, one would usually assume that the question turned not on whether the children themselves contracted, or gave a mandate, for X to occur, but rather on whether it was in their *interests* (or in the interests of society in general) that it should occur. That is, we normally suppose that (because of their age, inexperience, etc.) we have some sort of mandate from, or contract with, those 'in care', whereby we decide what they should do and what should happen to them on the basis of their own and the general interest, in return for which we look after them and do our best for them. (Similar points apply to colonial peoples, lunatics, etc.)

The question would therefore presumably be settled by those to whom the mandate is granted: that is, parents and teachers. This would not preclude them from giving the children freedom to decide and contract for themselves on the matter of moral assessment. In general, one would hope that, because of the immense importance of the subject, they and other Ses would agree to as much assessment as possible. It may be that we can, eventually, do without these *prima facie* 'difficult' or 'objectionable' methods of assessment. But we cannot assume this, and we ought not to forswear them in advance and 'on principle'.

1. Winch (1958), p. 123.

# Appendix B

# Knowing one's own emotions [EMP (1)]

Some philosophers[1] hold, or appear to hold, that one knows one's own emotions 'without observation'. On this view, if I am angry or frightened, perhaps there is no question of my having or lacking an *ability to identify* these emotions in myself: I just *know* I am. Of course, I may not tell you what I am feeling: I may lie, report insincerely. But there may be no question of my being mistaken, of my being more or less *good at* identifying what I feel. If I have understood this view correctly, it suggests that there is no such thing as EMP(1): although there can be EMP(2), for I ascribe specific emotions to other people on the basis of observation—I can identify them, make mistakes, sometimes know and sometimes don't know, can be more or less good at telling what they feel; but not (it may be said) in my own case.

Insofar as I understand this view, I disagree with it: briefly, because I don't think we normally use the word 'know' where there is no question of being mistaken, not having or having *grounds* for knowledge, evidence, etc. (Usages like 'knowing his own mind' are idiomatic, and do not appear in some other languages: this means something like 'having clear/fixed intentions and feelings', 'not dithering'.) But this is not the place to state my disagreement coherently and at length. Fortunately, I am excused from doing so because there *is* a sense of 'know' (I would say, the normal sense), roughly equivalent to 'identify', in which people can be said to be better or worse (to have more or less ability) at knowing what they themselves feel, in specific situations.

A paradigm case of this would be a man in a raging temper: 'I'm *not* angry!', he shouts, and he believes it. There is no question of insincerity: nor necessarily even of anything one could seriously call 'self-deception'. 'Me jealous of my husband's secretary?', says the wife, 'Good heavens, no! What *can* you mean by saying I hate and fear her?' There may be self-deception here, but in a clear sense she does not know that she is jealous, but *we* know. How do

---

1. E.g. Strawson (1967); Malcolm (1967), pp. 374–76, seems better.

we know? Just as we know the man is angry. We see his symptoms and behaviour, and perhaps we know from this or other occasions what he believes (that X has done him down, or stands in his way).

No doubt these people may have said to themselves ('said-in-their-hearts', as one author puts it[1]) at some time—perhaps very quickly—something like 'Damn the man, how maddening he is!' or 'Curse her; she's taking my husband away from me!' No doubt, if they kept their minds clear, they would be in a better position than we are to know that *this* is what they said to themselves (though not, I believe, 'without observation' of any kind). But the point remains that *now* they do not know, and we do.

In these cases, it seems plain that one reason why they do not know is that they lack a general ability. Part of this ability, indeed, may be involved in what I have called 'keeping one's mind clear'—not covering up or forgetting what one has said-in-one's-heart. But, just as obviously, these people could perfectly well *find out* that they were angry and jealous. They have only to look at their symptoms and behaviour, as we look at them. No doubt they have the concept of anger and jealousy all right, but they lack the 'recognition' abilities. They are bad at recognizing symptoms and behaviour, at correlating them and appreciating that they form an instance of 'anger' or 'jealousy'. Of course, they may also be *unwilling to use* this ability [in our language, they lack KRAT(1) (TT)]; but they may also be *unable*, to a greater or lesser extent. The distinction may be very hard to draw in practice. But we shall only deny the existence of an ability here if we insist that the *only* (logically possible) type of failure is a failure in sincerity, a failure to 'own up' —which would be classified as unwillingness rather than inability. Certainly, this is a very important type of failure; but it is not the only one.

To make the point in an extreme way: if I provide the angry man with a mirror in which he may see his facial expressions, or with a machine which rings a bell when his adrenalin-count rises steeply, I may not thereby increase his willingness to face and identify his anger—but I have certainly made it easier for him, or increased his ability, to do so. Similarly, if I train him in certain ways— perhaps in particular to 'search his mind' and *remember* what he has said-in-his-heart, in the way advocated by some psychologists— this may also increase his ability.

It may be said that these are rare cases, that although on some occasions one does not know what one feels, one usually or charac-

1. Kenny (1963).

teristically does. With this I have no quarrel. But—speaking again from the assessor's viewpoint, and with no desire to plunge into the philosophical complexities—I think it rash to demarcate any area where we can simply *assume* EMP(1) in the sense of knowledge-without-observation to exist, or where we can simply deny EMP(1) in the sense of knowledge-with-observation. For it seems to me that, where there is *any* question of S's stating or *reporting* his feelings (as opposed simply to *evincing* them), then there is also room for the concepts of evidence, verification and error. If S has just said-in-his-heart 'Would that my ship would come home!'—and there is no question of knowledge here, for this does not even look like a report or an assertion—and someone immediately asks him what he feels, S is hardly likely to forget what he has just said-in-his-heart, and will no doubt correctly report 'I was hoping that . . .'. The room for error is small. But insofar as S is reporting, the room is here.

How good various Ses are at correctly reporting, or knowing, their own feelings seems to me to be an empirical question, and empirical research might well show that they are less good than we might have thought. Even if I am wrong, such research might serve the function of making certain conceptual points about self-knowledge clearer to us. If I have overlooked or misunderstood those points, at least the researcher's time will not have been entirely wasted.

# 'Theories of moral development'

I have said little or nothing in this book about any 'theory' (or theories) of 'moral development'. This is partly because I have been exclusively concerned with assessment; but chiefly because it seems to me quite clear that all such theories are at best muddled, and at worst vacuous. I will try to justify this briefly.

1. First, and most important, 'moral development' is a name for nothing clear, as the reader will have gathered from earlier chapters. This in two ways. (a) Psychologists mean very different things by 'moral', and are usually not clear what they do mean. (b) On any conception of morality, a large number of *very different* qualities— skills, abilities, know-how, attitudes, etc.—enter into the picture. No *one* theory could possibly account for all these, any more than a single 'theory of learning' (another absurdity) could cover the logically different cases of learning chess, how to ride a bicycle, how to speak French, and how to talk. Obviously these different things 'develop' (or are learned, or acquired, or generated—we should not know what word to use until we were clearer about the phenomenon we were trying to explain) from different causes and at different rates. Even a rough trichotomy between moral judgement, moral feelings or dispositions, and moral behaviour is far too rough, as I hope our list of moral components has made clear.

2. Secondly, we are not clear which known aspects of child development we are going to count as relevant, and which irrelevant, to 'moral development', nor which we are going to count as falling within, and which outside, the concept. For example, the physical growth of the brain is obviously relevant to moral judgement-making: it might, in some degree, be not only relevant but a necessary precondition. But brain-development is not part of the concept of 'moral development'. Again, we might feel that a person's height or weight is irrelevant; but plainly his moral outlook on life may well be affected if he is very tall or short, fat or thin. Unless we *begin* by getting some firmer grasp on the overriding syllogisms or motivation-types that affect human thought and action, we cannot settle the question, and this implies, as I and others have

argued elsewhere (Wilson, 1972; Harré and Secord, 1972), a very different approach from that usually adopted by most psychologists.

3. Thirdly, we have no clear picture of the causal interaction of different types of development. Most 'theories of development' have arisen from the theorist focusing attention on one type of phenomenon ('identification', 'temptation-resistance', 'cognitive conflict', etc.): these theories are then seen (again like 'learning theories') as in some way competitors. Since we are not at all clear even that the phenomena are different, we are not likely to be clear about the layers and time-schemes in which they might properly be structured, or how they are causally related. Is it possible for children to care for others (PHIL) before they know what others feel (EMP)? Hot must the concept of a person arise in a child's mind? These are, as always, partly logical and partly empirical questions. Here again, I do not say that much of the psychological data we have is now interesting and relevant: I say only that its relevance is not clear, and that we are in no position to have anything we could seriously call a 'theory'.

Some philosophers may feel that enough is known to make some attempt at a unified theory, or, at least, to try to show in some detail just what aspects of morality research findings are relevant *to*. I am not so optimistic. The trouble is not just the complexities of the subject in general: it is also that even a single research finding often shows nothing clear, since it is nearly always unco-ordinated by other researches *on the same Ses* which alone would enable us to say exactly what had been discovered. We might hope for something from those psychologists who have paid more attention to this point, and to human rationality in general: these would be, for the most part, clinical psychologists and psychotherapists in the Freudian tradition. It is indeed true that post-Freudian pictures of 'development' seem to merit that title more than most pictures: we are given a story of successive object-relationships which are presented as virtually inevitable for the child, yet still given a story in which the child figures as a person rather than a behaviouristic machine. I personally find much in such pictures convincing; but the trouble is here that the basic evidence (or some of it) is not open to public inspection, and there is a lack of any scientific controls. Nevertheless, as has been very clearly argued (Harré and Secord, 1972), future research lies more on these lines than any others.

In the meantime, it seems plain that only much closer co-operation between empirical researchers and philosophers is likely to produce dividends. I have argued this more generally and at length elsewhere (Wilson, 1972), and will not repeat it here. But I do not think there is any alternative, nor any short cut to satisfactory results. The picture of psychologists conducting long, expensive and conceptually muddled researches, while sharp-shooting philosophers fire on them from a distance, is surely by now intolerable. Even when a competent philosopher does his best to criticise co-operatively (e.g. Peters in Mischel, 1972), it is plain that the gulf is appallingly wide, and should have been bridged at a far earlier stage of research. I hope, therefore, that here again I may be forgiven for not appearing to give 'theories of moral development' the attention they may seem to merit; for I believe that a fresh start is required, together with a good deal of conceptually satisfactory research, before we can begin to see clearly just how the (doubtless important) findings of existing researchers contribute to our overall picture. Until then we are whistling in the twilight, if not the dark.

# Further reading

In this field, where clarity is all-important, the inexperienced reader would be ill-advised to plough through a long list of books; and the experienced researcher will already be familiar with the literature. I shall simply mention a very few books relevant to different parts of this area, which (in my judgement) are clearly written and do not contain too much nonsense. The reader may glean from these all further references that he needs.

## 1. Psychology

Easily the best general guide is:

WRIGHT, D. (1971). *The Psychology of Moral Behaviour*. London: Penguin Books.

Two others are also worth mentioning:

GRAHAM, D. (1972). *Moral Learning and Development*. London: Batsford.
WILLIAMS, N. (1970). *The Moral Development of Children*. London: Macmillan.

All these give full references to the work of Piaget, Kohlberg and others.

## 2. Philosophy of psychology

Probably the best book to start with (because the simplest) is:

WILSON, J. (1972). *Philosophy and Educational Research*. Slough: NFER.

But the finest work on the whole topic is without doubt:

HARRÉ, R. and SECORD, P. F. (1972). *The Explanation of Social Behaviour* Oxford: Blackwell.

Other useful books include:

KENNY, A. (1963). *Action, Emotion and Will*. London: Routledge.
PETERS, R. S. (1958). *The Concept of Motivation*. London: Routledge.
WINCH, P. (1958). *The Idea of a Social Science*. London: Routledge.

## 3. Moral education

The conceptual foundations of research in this area are given in:

WILSON, J., WILLIAMS, N. and SUGARMAN, B. (1968). *Introduction to Moral Education*. London: Penguin Books.
WILSON, J. (1961). *Education in Religion and the Emotions*. London: Heinemann.

More general and wide-ranging discussions are to be found in:

SIZER, T. (Ed.) (1970). *Moral Education*. Cambridge, Mass.: Harvard University Press.

BECK, C. M., CRITTENDEN, B. S., and SULLIVAN, E. V. (Eds.) (1971). *Moral Education*. Toronto: University of Toronto Press.

The reader who is concerned with more detailed information about research, test-materials, and practical methods in this area is advised to consult two institutions in particular:

*The Warborough Research Unit*, c/o J. Wilson, Oxford University Dept. of Educational Studies, 15 Norham Gardens, Oxford, UK.

*The Ontario Institute for Studies in Education*, Bloor St., Toronto, Canada.

## References

ARISTOTLE (translated by J. A. K. Thomson) (1953). *Nicomachean Ethics*. London: Penguin Books.

BECK, C. M., CRITTENDEN, B. S. and SULLIVAN, E. V. (Eds.) (1971). *Moral Education*. Toronto: Toronto University Press.

BENNETT, J. (1964). *Rationality*. London: Routledge.

BLACK, M. (1967). 'Rules and Routines'. In: *The Concept of Education*, R. S. Peters (Ed.). London: Routledge.

BULL, N. J. (1969). *Moral Judgment from Childhood to Adolescence*. London: Routledge.

DEARDEN, R. F. (1968). *The Philosophy of Primary Education*. London: Routledge.

HARE, R. M. (1952). *The Language of Morals*. Oxford: Oxford University Press.

HARE, R. M. (1963). *Freedom and Reason*. Oxford: Oxford University Press.

HARRÉ, R. and SECORD, P. F. (1972). *The Explanation of Social Behaviour*. Oxford: Blackwell.

HARTSHORNE, H. and MAY, M. A. (1928–30). *Studies in the Nature of Character*, 3 vols. New York: Macmillan.

HAVIGHURST, R. J. and TABA, H. (1949). *Adolescent Character and Personality*. New York: Wiley.

KENNY, A. (1963). *Action, Emotion and Will*. London: Routledge.

KOHLBERG, L. (1964). 'The Development of Moral Character'. In: *Review of Child Development Research*, Hoffman, M. L. and Hoffman, L. W. (Eds.). New York: Russell Sage Foundation.

KOHLBERG, L. (1970). 'Education for Justice'. In: *Moral Education*, Sizer, T. (Ed.). Cambridge, Mass.: Harvard University Press.

KOHLBERG, L. (1971). 'Stages of Moral Development as a basis for Moral Education'. In: *Moral Education*, Beck, C. M., Crittenden, B. S. and Sullivan, E. V. (Eds.). Toronto: University of Toronto Press.

MACAULAY, J. and BERKOWITZ, L. (Eds.) (1970). *Altruism and Helping Behaviour*. New York: Academic Press.

MALCOLM, N. (1967). 'Knowledge of Other Minds'. In: *Essays in Philosophical Psychology*, Gustafson, D. F. (Ed.). London: Macmillan.

MURDOCH, I. (1970). *The Sovereignty of Good*. London: Routledge.

PECK, R. H. and HAVIGHURST, R. J. (1960). *The Psychology of Character Development*. New York: Wiley.

PETERS, R. S. (1966). *Ethics and Education*. London: Allen and Unwin.

PETERS, R. S. (1971). 'Moral Developments: A Plea for Pluralism'. In: *Cognitive Development and Epistemology*, Mischel, R. (Ed.). New York: Academic Press.

STRAWSON, P. F. (1967). 'Persons'. In: *Essays in Philosophical Psychology*, Gustafson, D. F. (Ed.). London: Macmillan.

WILLIAMS, N. (1969). 'Children's Moral Thought'. In: *Moral Education*, 1, 1 and 2. Oxford: Pergamon Press.

WILLIAMS, N. (1970). *The Moral Development of Children*. London: Macmillan.

WILSON, J., WILLIAMS, N. and SUGARMAN, B. (1968). *Introduction to Moral Education*. London: Penguin Books.

WILSON, J. (1971). *Education in Religion and the Emotions*. London: Heinemann.

WILSON, J. (1972). *Philosophy and Educational Research*. Slough: NFER.

WINCH, P. (1958). *The Idea of a Social Science*. London: Routledge.

WINCH, P. (1959). 'Nature and Convention'. In: *Proceedings of the Aristotelian Society*, 1959–60. London: Harrison and Sons.

WRIGHT, D. (1971). *The Psychology of Moral Behaviour*. London: Penguin Books.